The Power of Becoming

Steps to Your Best Self

By

Daniel Meguille

© Copyright 2025 Daniel Meguille. All rights reserved.

It is illegal to reproduce, duplicate or transmit any part of this document in either electronic means or printed format. Recording of this publication is strictly prohibited.

Dedication

To my second family: Layla Ali Dorre, Sahra Osman Mohammed, Anisa Mohamed, and Ryaan Abdurahman of RayRay Care Relief Ltd.

This book, *The Power of Becoming*, is lovingly dedicated to each of you. Our journey began as colleagues brought together by work, routine, and responsibility. Yet, as time passed and challenges arose, something far greater emerged: a bond defined by trust, respect, laughter, and an unwavering belief in one another's potential.

Each of you, in your own unique way, has contributed to my growth. Through your encouragement, honesty, and support, you pushed me beyond my comfort zone and helped me recognise the possibilities that lie within dedication and self-belief. You reminded me that personal transformation is not a solitary journey, but one shaped by the people who walk beside us - those who gently challenge us, celebrate our progress, and stand firm in moments of doubt.

- **Layla**, your strength and determination have inspired me to persevere, even when the path felt uncertain.
- **Sahra**, your compassion and clarity have helped me see purpose where I once saw obstacles.
- **Anisa**, your consistency and warmth have been a grounding force throughout this journey.
- **Ryaan**, your humour, insight, and sincerity have brought light and balance to even the most demanding days.

Together, you have helped me develop my skills, refine my character, and become the person I am today. The lessons I have learned from working alongside you—collaboration, resilience, loyalty, and faith—are woven throughout the pages of this book.

Thank you for being more than colleagues.

Thank you for believing in me.

Thank you for becoming family.

This book is as much yours as it is mine.

Acknowledgments

I extend my heartfelt gratitude to everyone who has played a part, directly or indirectly, in the creation of this book. *The Power of Becoming: Steps to Your Best Self* is the outcome of countless experiences, reflections, and lessons shaped by the people who have crossed my path and contributed to my growth.

To the individuals who have supported me with encouragement, honesty, and genuine friendship — thank you. Your consistency, wisdom, and positivity strengthened my resolve, sharpened my thinking, and inspired many of the insights captured within these pages. I am deeply grateful for the trust, respect, and companionship we have shared over the years.

I also wish to acknowledge the colleagues, mentors, and peers who have contributed to my personal and professional development. Your guidance and constructive feedback have helped me refine my skills, deepen my understanding, and continue striving for excellence in all that I do.

To my readers, thank you for choosing to embark on this journey of growth with me. Your decision to pursue transformation and self-improvement is both powerful and courageous. I hope the pages of this book offer clarity, inspiration, and the strength to seek the best version of yourself with determination and purpose.

Finally, I give thanks to everyone who has influenced my life's direction, whether through support, challenge, or inspiration. Each encounter has played a part in shaping the message of this book and the individual I continue to become.

Thank you for being part of this journey.

About the Author

Daniel Meguille is a committed leader, educator, and personal development practitioner whose work spans health and social care, leadership, safeguarding, and professional training. Over the years, Daniel has built a strong reputation for inspiring growth in others, guiding individuals to recognise their strengths, develop resilience, and pursue their highest potential with clarity and purpose.

His career has positioned him at the forefront of supporting learners, professionals, and organisations to improve practice, enhance well-being, and cultivate strong values. Daniel's approach blends practical experience with reflective insight, enabling him to connect deeply with people from all backgrounds. He believes that personal transformation begins with self-awareness, and that every individual has the capacity to evolve, improve, and shape the life they desire.

As a trainer, coach, and mentor, Daniel has supported countless individuals throughout their learning journeys, helping them build confidence, develop essential skills, and overcome internal barriers. His teaching style emphasises compassion, integrity, and the power of mindset — qualities that feature prominently throughout his work.

The Power of Becoming: Steps to Your Best Self represents the culmination of Daniel's passion for human growth. Drawing from his own experiences of challenge, reflection, and perseverance, he offers readers a practical and heartfelt guide to becoming the best version of themselves.

Beyond his professional roles, Daniel is a lifelong learner, reflective writer, and advocate for continuous improvement. He remains committed to empowering others to grow with courage, purpose, and authenticity, believing firmly that the journey of becoming never truly ends.

Contents

Preface 1
The Call to Growth 4
   The Inner Yearning for Change 4
   Breaking Free from Limiting Beliefs 10
   The First Steps Towards Growth 15
   How to Create Your Own Vision Board 18
Knowing Yourself 22
   Journalling: Your Personal Compass 22
   Strengths and Weaknesses: The Duality of Self 27
   Blind Spots: Unveiling the Hidden 32
Mindset Matters 37
   Understanding Fixed vs. Growth Mindset 37
   Cultivating Resilience Through Cognitive Shifts 40
   The Role of Affirmations 44
The Power of Habits 48
   Building Keystone Habits 48
   Creating Effective Rituals 53
   Staying Committed: Overcoming Resistance 57
Emotional Mastery 64
   Understanding Your Emotions 64
   Transforming Anxiety into Fuel 69
   Joy as a Practice 74
The Discipline of Focus 80
   Identifying Your Priorities 80
   Embracing Mindfulness 85
   Establishing Boundaries 91
The Strength of Character 97
   Defining Integrity and Its Role in Growth 97

- Building a Resilient Character 102
- The Courage to Stand Alone 108
- The Tapestry of Human Connection 114
- Setting Healthy Boundaries in Relationships 120
- Surrounding Yourself with Positivity 126

The Courage to Fail Forward 133
- Redefining Failure 133
- The Power of Recovery 138
- Creating a Culture of Learning 143

Discovering Your Why 150
- The Importance of Purpose 150
- Aligning Passions and Values 154
- Drafting Your Mission Statement 159
- Conclusion: The Ongoing Journey of Refinement 163

Contribution and Impact 164
- The Ripple Effect of Contribution 164
- Eliciting a Call to Service 170
- Legacy: The Long-Term Impacts 176

Becoming Never Ends 182
- Embracing Continuous Learning 182
- Celebrating Your Journey 188

Preface

Welcome to the wild ride that is *The Secrets of the Unseen*! Buckle up, because this isn't just another book; it's a journey into the unknown, a leap into the realms of mystery and wonder. Have you ever found yourself staring at the stars, pondering the vastness of the universe and the countless secrets hidden away from our sight? That's exactly how this book came to life. It all started one starlit night when a million questions buzzed in my mind, giving me that electrifying itch to uncover what lies beneath the surface of our everyday existence.

The research process was nothing short of an adventure. Imagine me, coffee in hand, diving deep into countless books, articles, and interviews with scientists, philosophers, and artists. Honestly, it was a whirlwind of inspiration! Each piece of information acted like a puzzle piece that slowly came together to form the vivid picture you'll soon explore. From the invisible forces that shape our world to the whispers of the universe that linger just beyond our perception, I wanted to encapsulate it all. This journey involved long nights of excitement—and a few existential crises, of course!

So, what can you expect? Expect to question everything you thought you knew about reality. Expect to feel your mind stretch and expand as you dive deep into realms where science meets the mystical. This isn't about wrapping everything up with a neat little bow; it's more like celebrating the beautiful chaos that is knowledge. Grab your favourite snack and prepare to challenge your perception of what you believe is real.

The Power of Becoming

As you flip through these pages, remember—you're not just reading; you're engaging in a conversation with the universe. We'll sidestep through history, tiptoe around scientific breakthroughs, and twirl joyfully in the mystical rain of thought-provoking ideas. I invite you to ponder, to marvel, and to question right along with me. Each chapter is designed to tug at the strings of your curiosity and leave you yearning for more.

Now, let's talk about the process. Creating *The Secrets of the Unseen* has been a labour of love—one that required not just research but a deep dive into my own thoughts and expectations. It meant peeling back layers of perception and challenging my own beliefs. The aim wasn't just to inform but to inspire a sense of wonder that would propel you forward in your exploration. After all, it's your journey just as much as it is mine!

I hope that by the time you reach the final page, you'll feel an exhilarating spark—a newfound appreciation for the invisible threads that weave our reality. Stay curious, challenge the status quo, and most importantly, let your imagination soar!

As we embark on this expedition through the unseen realms, I encourage you not to skip around or rush through the chapters. This isn't a sprint; it's a marathon of discovery. Let the words sink in, let the ideas swirl around your mind, and allow yourself the grace to revel in the unknown. It's perfectly OK to pause, breathe, and reflect as we journey together.

So, dear reader, are you ready? Are you geared up with an open mind and a curious heart? Let's dive into this adventure that promises not only to expand your knowledge but to ignite the fire of wonder that resides within you. I can't wait to see where this journey takes us!

With open arms and a sense of exhilaration, I invite you to turn the page and step into this marvellous world of secrets and revelations. Let the adventure begin—the universe awaits!

With excitement and wonder,

Daniel Meguille

The Call to Growth

The Inner Yearning for Change

The inner yearning for change is a familiar sensation—a whisper that often starts as a dull ache in our hearts and evolves into a powerful motivation urging us to seek something greater. It transcends age, culture, and circumstance, uniting us through a fundamental human experience: the recognition of our discontent.

This feeling may manifest as an unshakeable restlessness or the nagging thought that there must be more to life than the routine we have settled into. Psychological studies reveal that the desire for growth is deeply rooted in our very being. Research conducted by psychologists such as Abraham Maslow illustrates that the pursuit of self-actualisation—the process of realising our full potential—is a fundamental human drive.

The hierarchy of needs emphasises that once our basic needs for safety and belonging are met, the desire to grow and evolve becomes a powerful motivator. This yearning does not merely seek external achievements; it calls for internal transformation and enrichment.

Consider the story of Maria, a middle-aged bank manager. For years, she followed the scripted path laid out for her—working hard, earning promotions, and providing for her family. Yet after a decade in her role, a growing sense of unfulfilment began to envelop her.

It struck her during a quiet moment while driving home; the familiarity of her daily commute felt stifling rather than comforting. The realisation that she had drifted into a life defined by routine rather than passion unveiled an unsettling truth: Maria was not just seeking a new job; she was yearning for a complete reinvention of herself.

Most of us can resonate with moments like Maria's—instances in our lives when the comfort of routine clashes with a burgeoning desire for something more. This inconsistency often prompts deep reflection as we recognise that we are not merely creatures of habit but dynamic beings with the capacity for growth.

This inner conflict can serve as the first step in our journey of self-discovery and growth. Embracing this feeling of yearning allows us to identify and confront the aspects of our lives that no longer serve us.

The longing for change often appears in the unlikeliest of places. It may strike during mundane activities—while washing the dishes, waiting for a train, or attending a friend's wedding. A song on the radio can evoke memories of dreams deferred, igniting the inner voice that begs for action. This voice becomes almost magnetic, pulling us towards the possibility of transformation. Yet many choose to ignore it, fearing the changes it might demand.

In moments of contemplation, it can be helpful to visualise what this voice represents. Imagine a garden overgrown with weeds. The weeds symbolise old habits, fears, and doubts that take root in our lives, suffocating the growth potential. Beneath the surface, however, vibrant flowers—our dreams, passions, and aspirations—lie dormant, yearning for the right conditions to bloom. The inner yearning for change serves as the sunlight that makes these seeds sprout, urging us to untangle ourselves from the confines of our current existence.

The Power of Becoming

This metaphor resonates with many who have faced significant life changes. Take John, a once-eminent lawyer who, feeling shackled by the expectations placed upon him, found solace and clarity during a hiking trip in the mountains. It was there, surrounded by nature's beauty, that something profound occurred. He felt an overwhelming desire to write a book, despite having spent decades practising law—a profession that, while noble, left him feeling unfulfilled.

This yearning for change awakened something in him; it reminded him of the creative spark he had long ignored. Both Maria's and John's stories illustrate the essence of an inner yearning that demands attention. It beckons us to dig deeper, to confront any limiting beliefs that have taken root within us.

Each of us possesses values and dreams that lie dormant, waiting for the sunlight of self-discovery to help them flourish. Embracing this transformative yearning empowers us to ask: What do I truly want? What would it take for me to pursue that desire?

To further understand this yearning, consider the work of Brené Brown, a researcher in the field of vulnerability and courage. She emphasises that embracing our vulnerability is a pivotal step towards genuine growth. Acknowledging our desires and fears means allowing ourselves to be imperfect, opening up avenues for exploration. It is often in our moments of vulnerability that we connect most deeply to our inner yearning—those raw, authentic desires fuel our longing for change.

Yet despite its power, the yearning for growth can also stir up feelings of complacency and fear. It is not uncommon to feel paralysed by the weight of expectations, both self-imposed and societal. This internal struggle can lead individuals to retreat into comfort, fearing the disappointment that comes with the unknown.

The voice yearning for change may clash with deeper insecurities—the fear of failure or judgement, the worry that our aspirations are unattainable. Each of us holds within us a kaleidoscope of emotions and experiences shaped by our backgrounds, cultures, and belief systems.

This rich tapestry creates unique narratives that give form to our yearnings, but it can also blind us to our potential. Every person has a unique story filled with powerful lessons. Understanding your personal narrative is essential in igniting the journey toward change.

Reflecting on your life can be a catalyst for discovering aspects you wish to transform. Reflect on the times when you felt comfortable and confident, as well as moments of confusion or regret. Are there recurring themes? Perhaps they can illuminate the core desires that fuel your inner yearning.

Spend time thinking about what excites you, what makes you feel alive—even if it feels daunting to admit. For example, if you often feel envious when you see friends pursuing adventurous careers, it may indicate a longing for exploration within yourself. Maybe you've put aside a creative hobby for practicality's sake, but that inner voice insists on expressing itself through art or writing. Recognising these themes shifts the conversation from fear to opportunity.

The yearning for change often bubbles beneath the surface, fuelled by discontent with the status quo. It can present itself subtly, as an itch that demands to be scratched or as an ache for something more. But it serves as a potent invitation to explore the depths within.

As you begin to consider your own experiences, allow the yearning to surface fully—don't shy away from it. Embrace it as a signpost guiding you toward growth. Let that yearning resonate deeper.

Take a moment to journal about your feelings, pose questions to yourself, or engage with a trusted friend who can reflect your experiences. Each exploration can lead to revelations; the act of vocalising your desires instils power, creating benchmarks for your changing perspective.

The acknowledgement of your inner voice does not mean you must take immediate, drastic action; sometimes, simply recognising your yearnings is a critical step. It is within this understanding that our true exploration begins.

As you sit with these thoughts, consider allowing the yearning to become an ally rather than a fearsome foe. It reflects your potential and serves as a driver on your journey towards self-discovery.

In a society often focused on the external markers of success, the internal journey can become muted. The slow march of time can urge us into a groove, making it easy to dismiss the inner yearnings for change. It becomes imperative to recognise how the external world may try to shape our desires, but instead, tune into that quiet voice that speaks of what resonates with your authentic self.

As you move forward, remember that the process of growth and self-discovery is not a linear path. There will be moments of clarity, joy, confusion, and even regret along the way, but each experience serves as an important part of your narrative.

Practising self-compassion throughout this journey will permit you to explore freely without the shackles of perfectionism. The inner yearning for change is a call to tune into the significance of your story. It invites you to recognise that your growth and transformation are not only essential for yourself but also for those who surround you.

When you honour your desire for change, it creates a ripple effect, encouraging others to pursue their own paths to growth. As you stand at the precipice of consideration, invite yourself to reflect on the aspects of life you envision differently.

This is a crucial stage before diving deeper into self-discovery. Recognising what you wish to enhance or change allows your yearning for growth to gain clarity. It may also serve as a motivator to foster deeper exploration into your strengths, limitations, and passions.

Embrace this moment of reflection as a vital part of the broader framework of your journey to becoming your best self. Acknowledge that this inward exploration is necessary; it legitimises your yearning as a valuable compass directing you towards meaningful change.

Understanding your inner yearning for change can become a profound awakening. Recognise its persistence and appreciate the humble urgency it instils. As you equip yourself with this awareness, you set the stage for growth, transformation, and an extraordinary journey of becoming.

The inner voice that yearns for change is never wrongly attuned—it merely seeks the space to blossom into fruition. So, take heed of its call, initiate self-reflection, and prepare to explore the landscapes of your evolving self. The journey ahead promises to be enriching, monumental, and essential.

Breaking Free from Limiting Beliefs

Breaking free from limiting beliefs is akin to shedding layers of heavy garments that have been draped over our shoulders since childhood. These beliefs often manifest as invisible chains that bind us, preventing us from realising our true potential and achieving the life we desire.

As we explore this essential aspect of personal growth, we will uncover the various types of limiting beliefs, examine their origins, and, most importantly, share stories of individuals who identified and overcame these barriers, allowing their true selves to shine forth.

To begin, let's define what limiting beliefs are. They are the assumptions or convictions that we hold about ourselves and the world around us. They dictate what we think we can accomplish and, more critically, what we believe we cannot do. These beliefs are often formed in our formative years, influenced by family dynamics, early experiences, and the societal norms that pervade our environment. They can stem from deeply ingrained fear, the need for acceptance, or a misguided assessment of our capabilities.

Consider the classic example of a young girl named Emily. From a young age, Emily was told that she was not good at maths, a sentiment echoed by her teachers and reinforced by her peers. Over the years, this belief became entrenched in her psyche. When it came time to choose her subjects in high school, she predefined her path, steering clear of anything that involved numbers. She pursued subjects that were "safer" and aligned with her perceived capabilities, yet deep down, she yearned to explore her potential in STEM.

It wasn't until her final year at university, after connecting with a supportive mentor who encouraged her to take a calculus class, that Emily broke free from this limiting belief. To her surprise, she excelled in her maths class, developing a newfound love for problem-solving and analytical thinking. This transformation shifted her trajectory, opening doors to career paths she had once considered impossible.

Emily's story is not unique. It reflects the experiences of many individuals who have succumbed to the whispering doubts fostered by their upbringing or environment.

Limiting beliefs manifest in various ways, and their impact can be profound:

1. **Self-doubt** – The most pervasive limiting belief, self-doubt insists that we are not enough: not intelligent, talented, deserving, or capable. This inner critic can sabotage opportunities and lead to resignation.

2. **Fear of judgement** – Often rooted in the fear of rejection, this belief paralyses individuals, causing them to avoid situations where they might be evaluated or criticised. For example, a talented writer like Michael may avoid sharing his work, convinced that others will not appreciate or validate his effort.

3. **Fixed identity** – This belief defines us by our past experiences or mistakes, often rendering us unwilling to move forward and evolve. A person may think, "I have always been shy; I cannot become more outgoing," effectively shackling themselves to a narrow identity.

4. **Scarcity mindset** – The conviction that resources are limited can prevent us from pursuing opportunities or taking risks. An entrepreneur might obsess over competition rather than recognising the market potential and their unique contribution.

5. **Unworthiness** – Many individuals believe they don't deserve happiness or success due to past failures or the perception that they are less deserving than others. This sense of unworthiness can thwart relationships, careers, and personal fulfilment.

Understanding the origins of limiting beliefs is essential in disentangling ourselves from their grip. Many such beliefs are formed during childhood, a phase of life characterised by immense vulnerability and receptiveness. Children absorb messages from parents, teachers, and peers without the critical lens they develop later in life. For instance, a child who is often criticised for their efforts may grow into an adult who hesitates to take risks for fear of making mistakes.

Moreover, societal expectations and cultural narratives also shape beliefs. In many cultures, certain roles or careers are deemed acceptable for specific genders or socioeconomic backgrounds, prompting individuals to conform rather than forge their own paths.

These deeply ingrained norms can perpetuate limiting beliefs that constrain potential.

The journey towards breaking free from limiting beliefs often begins with awareness. Identifying these beliefs requires introspection and honesty. Reflect on your reactions to challenges, your self-talk during moments of doubt, and the situations where you feel restricted.

Ask yourself: What beliefs do I hold about my abilities? Where do these beliefs stem from? Have I ever questioned their validity?

Facing such questions may lead to discovering beliefs that have long dictated your choices. Perhaps you've always avoided public speaking because you believe you're not articulate enough, or maybe you've hesitated to apply for that promotion because you think you're not qualified. Acknowledging these beliefs is the first step towards dismantling them.

Once you have identified your limiting beliefs, visualisation can be a powerful tool for transformation. Visualise a life where these constraints do not exist. Picture yourself pursuing new opportunities, taking risks, and embracing challenges without the shadow of doubt. Imagine what it would look like to step into your fullest potential without the gnaw of fear or insecurity holding you back.

Consider the story of James, a successful project manager who once felt inadequate because he had never completed his university education. For years, he found himself second-guessing his expertise, especially when leading teams. He often deferred to others' opinions out of fear of being perceived as less competent.

The Power of Becoming

Yet he was a natural leader, skilled in managing projects and motivating his teammates.

With encouragement from a trusted colleague, James began to visualise his leadership style. He realised his self-worth did not hinge on formal education but on the skills he had developed through years of hands-on experience. By visualising himself confidently leading meetings and making critical decisions, he began to act in ways that reflected this new belief. Over time, he became the go-to person when stakeholders sought insights. The shift in his mindset was not instant, but by gradually aligning his actions with his latent beliefs, he transformed into a confident leader who contributed significantly to his organisation.

For many, the process of dismantling limiting beliefs may require additional support. Seeking mentorship, engaging in personal development workshops, or finding accountability partners can encourage necessary to challenge and reframe these beliefs. Sharing your experiences with others allows you to recognise that you are not alone in your struggles. Connection is a powerful antidote to the isolation that limiting beliefs can induce.

As you embark on this journey, it is crucial to celebrate small victories. Breaking free from limiting beliefs is not about reaching an end goal; it is about reshaping the journey itself. Each step counts, whether it is voicing your opinion in a meeting, applying for a job you once thought unattainable, or simply challenging negative self-talk. Recognising progress builds momentum and fosters a growth-oriented mindset that propels you forward.

The stories of others who have conquered their limiting beliefs can serve as inspiration in your journey. Take the instance of Sarah, a woman who once believed she could never run a marathon. Having struggled with body-image issues for much of her life, she thought this physical feat was beyond her reach. However, in her thirties, she decided to start jogging. At first, her goals were modest—she aimed to run for a few minutes without stopping. As her stamina grew, so did her confidence. With each accomplishment, whether running a mile or completing a charitable 5K, Sarah transformed her self-image. Eventually, she set her sights on a marathon and trained diligently, ultimately completing it.

Sarah's journey illustrates that our perceived limits can stretch far beyond what our minds initially dictate.

In closing, as we reflect on the concept of limiting beliefs, it becomes clear that these invisible chains do not have to define our lives. By understanding their origins, identifying them within ourselves, and visualising a future unbounded by these constraints, we empower ourselves to embark on a journey of growth.

Take the time to reflect on the beliefs that hold you back. Which stories have you been telling yourself? Are they rooted in truth or in fear? As you venture forth, ask yourself: What would my life look like if I shattered these limitations?

The answers may inspire a path you never thought possible—one that invites you on the exhilarating journey of becoming your best self. Embrace the challenge and allow the power of becoming to illuminate the road ahead.

The First Steps Towards Growth

The journey towards personal growth begins with understanding that change is not only possible but necessary for a fulfilling life.

The Power of Becoming

Recognising the call to growth is a vital first step, and this section aims to provide you with actionable steps to initiate this transformative journey.

Before diving into practical tools and exercises, it's essential to spend some time in reflection. Reflection allows us to pause, assess our current situation, and evaluate what needs to change. This period of introspection can be both enlightening and motivational, laying the groundwork for the goal-setting that follows.

To begin, find a quiet space where you can think without distraction. Take a moment to breathe deeply, bringing your awareness to the present. Ask yourself the following questions:

- What aspects of my life feel stagnant or unfulfilling?
- Are there dreams I've put on hold or goals I've never pursued?
- What would my life look like if I were actively engaged in pursuing my passions and aspirations?

After reflecting on these questions, capture your thoughts in a journal. Writing your feelings and ideas down not only helps to organise your thoughts but also solidifies your commitment to change.

Once you have reflected on your current state, the next step is to set goals. Setting clear, actionable goals is crucial for your growth journey, as it transforms abstract desires into concrete plans of action. One effective framework for this is the **SMART** criteria, which stands for *Specific, Measurable, Achievable, Relevant,* and *Time-bound.*

Let's break down each component:

1. **Specific** – A specific goal clearly defines what you want to accomplish. Instead of saying, "I want to be healthier," you might say, "I want to exercise three times a week for thirty minutes."

2. **Measurable** – Incorporating measurable criteria allows you to track your progress. Using the same example, you can mark your workouts on a calendar.

3. **Achievable** – Ensure that the goal is realistic and attainable given your current resources and constraints. It's important to challenge yourself, but setting an impossible goal can lead to discouragement.

4. **Relevant** – Your goal should align with your broader life objectives and values. Ask yourself, "Does this goal resonate with who I am or who I aspire to be?"

5. **Time-bound** – Setting a deadline creates a sense of urgency and prompts consistent action. Specify when you aim to achieve your goal—whether in one month, six months, or a year.

Now that you understand the SMART framework, try applying it to a goal you identified during reflection. For instance, if you feel you need to improve your public-speaking skills, a SMART goal could be:

"I will join a local Toastmasters club within the next two weeks to enhance my speaking abilities and deliver a speech by the end of next month."

Next, let's explore the concept of vision boards. A vision board is a powerful visual tool that can help manifest your goals and aspirations. It acts as a constant reminder of what you are working towards, reinforcing motivation and commitment.

How to Create Your Own Vision Board

1. **Gather materials** – You'll need a board (such as a poster, corkboard, or digital platform), magazines, pictures, quotes, scissors, and glue. For a digital approach, numerous apps and websites can facilitate this.

2. **Visual confirmation of goals** – As you cut out images and quotes, think about what resonates with you and represents your ambitions.

3. **Arrange your board** – Place the images and quotes on your board without fixing them initially. Rearrange until the design feels right.

4. **Affix your inspirations** – Once satisfied, secure everything to your board.

5. **Display your board** – Put it somewhere you will see it daily. Regular exposure strengthens subconscious reinforcement of your intentions.

Alongside your vision board, engage with practical exercises to create a more structured growth map. One effective exercise is performing a **SWOT analysis** on yourself—identifying your *Strengths, Weaknesses, Opportunities,* and *Threats.*

1. **Strengths** – What are your key skills, talents, experiences, and resources? These form the backbone of your growth.

2. **Weaknesses** – Consider areas where you feel challenged or lack proficiency. Self-awareness is a cornerstone of development.

3. **Opportunities** – Identify external factors that can aid your growth, such as classes, workshops, mentors, or networks.

4. **Threats** – Recognise obstacles such as time constraints or negative influences. Awareness allows you to develop strategies to overcome them.

After completing your SWOT analysis, summarise your findings in a way that aligns with your goals. This clarity will be invaluable as you chart your path forward.

When creating your growth map, break larger goals into smaller, manageable steps. This approach—often referred to as micro-goals—allows for gradual progress and prevents overwhelm. For example, if your larger goal is to write a book, a micro-goal could be writing for thirty minutes daily or completing a chapter within a set timeframe.

Incorporate regular review and reflection. Schedule periodic check-ins with yourself to assess progress. This not only keeps you accountable but also provides valuable opportunities to celebrate small wins or adjust your approach as needed.

Ask yourself:

- What progress have I made towards my goals?

The Power of Becoming

- What challenges have I faced, and how can I overcome them?

- How do I feel about my journey?

- What adjustments do I need to make moving forward?

These reflections maintain a sense of agency and ownership over your growth process, ensuring you're consciously steering your path.

Visual aids can further enhance engagement. Use charts or timelines to symbolise milestones; these reminders reinforce positivity and perseverance.

Technology can also support your journey. Goal-tracking apps, journalling tools, or online communities can offer accountability and fresh perspectives.

Finally, foster a sense of empowerment as you embark on this path. Remind yourself that you hold the reins. Change may feel daunting, but every small step is progress. Adopt a mindset of resilience and openness to new possibilities.

As you set forth on your path to growth, visualise who you want to become. Engage with affirmations and positive self-talk that bolster confidence and emotional well-being. The journey of becoming is about embracing who you are while patiently working towards who you wish to be.

Remember, the steps you take today lay the foundation for your future. Growth isn't merely about reaching a destination; it's about the journey itself. Embrace discomfort and uncertainty—they are signs that you are evolving.

The first steps towards growth involve a dynamic interplay of reflection, goal-setting, visualisation, and action. By engaging in these practices, you create a map for your journey that provides both direction and motivation. Recognise that each choice you make moves you closer to your best self.

The power of becoming lies within you. Now is the time to ignite that power and take the first steps towards a brighter future.

Knowing Yourself

Journalling: Your Personal Compass

Journalling has emerged as a vital practice for self-discovery, serving as a personal compass that directs us towards deeper understanding and awareness of ourselves. In the fast-paced modern world, where distractions are abundant and noise often drowns out the voice within, the simple act of writing can be a grounding force. It provides an opportunity to explore our thoughts, feelings, and experiences in a safe, judgement-free space.

Through the act of journalling, we can delve into the layers of our personality, uncovering hidden aspirations, fears, desires, and values. Reflective writing and stream-of-consciousness exercises are two effective techniques that can facilitate this journey. Reflective writing encourages us to ponder our experiences, drawing connections between the past and present, and helping us make sense of our lives. It prompts us to ask critical questions: What did I learn from this experience? How has it shaped who I am? Through this form of writing, we can extract valuable lessons, allowing our experiences to inform our future choices.

Stream-of-consciousness writing, on the other hand, is less structured and more spontaneous in nature. It is about letting the words flow without censoring our thoughts. This technique can be cathartic, revealing our subconscious mind and allowing us to tap into emotions and ideas that we may not have been consciously aware of. By setting aside judgement and simply writing whatever comes to mind, we can often unearth insights that pinpoint our deepest fears or long-held aspirations.

The Power of Becoming

For instance, consider the power of a simple prompt such as, "What do I most fear about pursuing my dreams?" As you begin to write, you might find yourself expressing feelings you have not fully acknowledged. Perhaps you fear failure, or maybe the idea of success seems overwhelming. Journalling allows you to articulate these fears and grasp the obstacles standing in the way of your aspirations. This clarity can be the first step towards navigating these fears, transforming them from vague anxieties into tangible challenges that can be confronted and addressed.

One of the most profound aspects of journalling is the dialogue it cultivates with ourselves. When we write, we are not just recording thoughts; we are engaging in a conversation. This self-dialogue can lead to remarkable insights. You may discover patterns in your thinking that you were previously unaware of, or connect the dots between various experiences that illuminate your path forward. For example, suppose you write about a recurring feeling of dissatisfaction at work. In that case, you might uncover a passion for creativity that you have long suppressed but that could lead you to a more fulfilling career.

Through ongoing journalling, you can start to identify your values—those core beliefs that guide your decisions and actions. By articulating what matters most to you, you create a map for your life, one that directs your choices and helps you remain true to yourself. For instance, you might find that themes of adventure, family, or personal growth appear frequently in your entries. Recognising these values provides clarity about what you want to prioritise in your life.

The Power of Becoming

To kick-start your journalling journey, consider these guided prompts designed to draw you into deeper reflection. Take your time with each of them, allowing your thoughts to unfold naturally.

1. "What are three experiences in my life that significantly shaped who I am today?"

2. "What dreams did I have as a child, and how do they compare to my current aspirations?"

3. "What are the most pressing fears I face, and what steps can I take to confront them?"

4. "Who embodies my ideal self, and what qualities do I admire in them?"

5. "What does success mean to me, and how does it differ from others' definitions of success?"

These prompts are not exhaustive, but they serve as launching pads for self-exploration. Spend time with each question and let your thoughts flow freely. There are no right or wrong answers, only your truth. Over time, as you revisit these questions and reflect on your responses, you will likely notice shifts in your understanding and perspective.

Journalling does not have to be a daily chore; it can be a natural extension of your thoughts and feelings. Some find it helpful to set aside a designated time each day, whereas others prefer to write when inspiration strikes. The format of your journal is entirely up to you. Whether you opt for a notebook, a digital platform, or even audio journalling, the key is consistency and authenticity.

The Power of Becoming

As you embark on this personal journey, remember that it is a practice, not a performance. Allow yourself the freedom to express your innermost thoughts without the pressure of perfection. Your journal is for your eyes only; it is a safe haven for exploration and experimentation. Over time, you will begin to notice how your writing influences your thoughts and actions. The act of putting pen to paper, or fingers to keys, can lead to greater clarity in decision-making and enhanced self-awareness. Each entry becomes a building block in the foundation of your understanding, paving the way for growth and transformation.

A common challenge when starting a journalling practice is the fear of judgement, whether self-judgement or concern about others potentially reading your thoughts. It is important to silence that inner critic. Remember, the purpose of journalling is self-exploration, not perfection. Allow your writing to be raw and honest, and recognise that your journal is a private space for you to explore your thoughts without fear. The authenticity you bring to your writing will enrich the insights you glean.

Embrace the messiness of your thoughts and feelings. You may write about your dreams one day and your frustrations the next. The undulating nature of consciousness is a fundamental aspect of being human, reflecting the complexity of our experiences. Allow this complexity to be part of your explorative journey.

As you evolve and your life circumstances change, your journalling will naturally adapt. You might find that your focus shifts from personal goals to relationships, health, or professional aspirations. This fluidity is a sign of growth, indicating that you are paying attention to your needs and desires as they evolve.

The Power of Becoming

Journalling is not a static practice; it is a living dialogue that evolves alongside you.

As you delve deeper, consider revisiting past entries. This can help you trace your personal evolution, revealing how far you have come and where you have grown. It can also bring to light unresolved themes or lingering emotions that may require further exploration. When you look back at what you have written, consider how your perspective has shifted over time. This reflection can serve as a reminder of your resilience and capacity for growth, reinforcing your commitment to becoming the best version of yourself.

Eventually, you may want to incorporate thematic journalling, selecting particular subjects or areas of focus to explore in depth. Whether you choose themes related to personal development, relationships, career aspirations, or emotional health, this targeted approach can spur even greater insights. For example, a month dedicated to exploring your relationship with fear might reveal patterns in how you respond to challenges and provide practical strategies for growth.

As you navigate this process, remember that journalling is an art that requires practice and patience. The more you engage with your journal, the more you will learn about yourself. Embrace the discomfort that arises during this exploration; it often signals the areas where growth is most needed. Your journal will provide a space for you to confront these truths and guide you toward solutions or new paths forward.

In a world inundated with external noise and influences, journalling creates an opportunity to connect with your inner voice. It empowers you to confront your truths, challenge limiting beliefs, and dream boldly about your future. Each word you write is an invitation to unfold layers of understanding that inform who you are and how you wish to engage with the world.

As this journey of self-discovery unfolds, remember that journalling is not an endpoint but a powerful tool on the path of becoming. It equips you with insights to navigate your journey, encouraging steps that align with your authentic self. Through exploration of your inner landscape, the clarity you gain will guide you in crafting a life that reflects your deepest values and aspirations.

In conclusion, journalling is a transformative practice that serves as a personal compass, leading you towards greater self-awareness and insight. By fostering a dialogue with yourself through reflective writing and stream-of-consciousness exercises, you can unveil the intricacies of your personality and illuminate your true self. Whether through guided prompts or spontaneous reflection, allow the act of writing to nurture your journey towards becoming your best self. Embrace this opportunity for exploration, and you may find that the journey ahead is not only revealing but profoundly enriching, setting the stage for a life lived with intention and purpose.

Strengths and Weaknesses: The Duality of Self

In our journey of becoming, understanding the duality of self, our strengths and weaknesses, plays a crucial role. This section guides you through recognising, accepting, and embracing both facets of your personality. Strengths and weaknesses exist in a continual interplay, shaping who we are and how we navigate the world. By illuminating this duality, we can encourage personal growth and fulfilment aligned with our true selves.

First, let us explore what constitutes a strength. A strength is often viewed as a natural talent, skill, or quality that enables us to perform tasks well and achieve desired outcomes. These aspects of ourselves evoke feelings of confidence and competence, energising us to face challenges. For instance, someone with strong communication skills may find fulfilment in professions that require constant engagement with others, while a person with a strategic mindset might thrive in roles that demand foresight and planning.

Strengths are not merely innate traits; they are also cultivated through experience, practice, and intention. Consider the musician who has honed their craft over years of dedicated work. Their technical skill is a strength, but it is also a reflection of persistence and passion. Recognising strengths affirms our capabilities and potential, encouraging us to nurture these qualities and leverage them in our pursuits.

Although acknowledging our strengths brings power, it is equally important to confront our weaknesses. A weakness may be described as a limitation or deficiency that hinders performance or growth. It can be uncomfortable to acknowledge these aspects, but avoidance only strengthens their hold. Embracing weaknesses does not equate to resignation or self-judgement; it fosters a deeper understanding of the whole self. This awareness creates space for growth, allowing us to work towards improvement while acknowledging that imperfection is an inherent part of being human.

A practical approach is the personal SWOT analysis, a strategic tool traditionally applied in business but equally useful for personal development. SWOT stands for Strengths, Weaknesses, Opportunities, and Threats. Conducting a personal SWOT analysis enables structured reflection on strengths and weaknesses while identifying opportunities available to you and potential threats you may face.

To begin, draw a large square and divide it into four equal quadrants. Label them "Strengths," "Weaknesses," "Opportunities," and "Threats." Engage with each section honestly.

- **Strengths**: List qualities, skills, and achievements that resonate with you. What do you excel at? What comes naturally? Consider feedback from friends, colleagues, or mentors that highlights your abilities.

- **Weaknesses**: Acknowledge areas where you face challenges or feel less confident, such as time management, procrastination, or lack of assertiveness. Identifying limitations allows you to take proactive steps to address them.

- **Opportunities**: Note external factors that could aid growth, such as courses, workshops, mentors, or networks. Consider how these align with your interests and strengths.

- **Threats**: Recognise external challenges, from industry competition to personal circumstances that inhibit growth. Awareness enables you to develop effective strategies that enhance your resilience.

Once complete, synthesise the insights from each quadrant. How do your strengths align with opportunities? Can you devise actions to confront weaknesses while mitigating threats? This analysis fosters understanding and guides deliberate steps on your path to becoming.

To illustrate, consider Jane, a marketing professional known for creativity and innovation. Jane recognised that one of her greatest strengths was thinking laterally, but she struggled to present ideas confidently in large meetings. Rather than avoid this weakness, she enrolled in public-speaking workshops and practised with supportive colleagues. Over time, she gained competence and confidence, sharing her ideas with senior management. By leveraging creativity while improving communication, she advanced her career and became a respected voice in her organisation.

Another example is Tom, an engineer skilled in problem-solving. His analytical prowess was his strongest asset, yet he struggled to connect with his team on an emotional level. Understanding that collaboration hinges on interpersonal skills, Tom sought feedback from peers and mentors. He recognised that his analytical focus left little room for emotional intelligence. Through workshops on active listening and emotional skills, he built healthier relationships with colleagues and stepped into leadership, harmonising technical expertise with an ability to inspire others.

These cases show how embracing the reality of our duality can lead to deeper self-awareness, growth, and fulfilment. Recognising strengths propels us forward, while consciously addressing weaknesses paves the way for richer, more meaningful connections with ourselves and others.

The path to self-awareness is not linear; it is punctuated by moments of triumph and vulnerability. As you continue to explore your own strengths and weaknesses, take note of the progress you make. Celebrate your strengths, and approach your weaknesses with compassion. They do not define your worth; they reveal areas ripe for growth.

Recognising and embracing your duality allows a more holistic view of self. Rather than striving for a one-dimensional narrative of either strong or weak, accept the complex interplay between these characteristics. This acceptance empowers you to create an authentic narrative that aligns with your aspirations and values.

Growth is a lifelong process that evolves as you do. Allow yourself to be a work in progress. Each decision, experience, and reflection contributes to the developing canvas of your life.

The power of becoming is rooted in knowing yourself. By embracing the duality of your strengths and weaknesses, you free yourself from perfectionism and harsh judgement. Every trait, positive or negative, contributes to your unique journey. In the tapestry of life, both the vibrant colours of your strengths and the shadows of your weaknesses work together to create a picture that is entirely and beautifully you.

In conclusion, as you embark on this path of self-discovery, conduct your personal SWOT analysis with honesty and an open heart. Use it to navigate your growth, celebrate achievements, and cultivate resilience in the face of challenges. The journey is as significant as the destination. By knowing yourself, both strengths and weaknesses, you empower your choices to align with your true essence, flourish as an individual, and contribute positively to those around you.

Blind Spots: Unveiling the Hidden

In the journey of becoming our best selves, one crucial aspect often remains overlooked: our blind spots. These are the unconscious biases, habits, and perspectives that we hold, which can hinder our growth and progress. While self-awareness is rightly celebrated as a foundational pillar of personal development, blind spots can create significant barriers to that very awareness. They can obscure our understanding of ourselves; without confronting them, we may continue down paths that no longer serve us. The exploration of blind spots is not merely an exercise in introspection; it is a vital element of the growth journey.

Blind spots exist in many forms. They can manifest as outdated beliefs, unproductive habits, or interpersonal behaviours that we may not recognise. Sometimes, our inability to see these blind spots arises from deep-seated confidence in our self-perception. We might believe we are open-minded or skilled communicators, only to discover, through feedback or reflection, that we fall short of our own ideals. The discomfort that comes with recognising these discrepancies is essential for transformation; this revelation opens the door to newfound growth and helps unlock our potential.

To begin unveiling these hidden aspects, we must engage in self-reflection and actively seek feedback from others. Self-reflection may include journalling or quiet contemplation, and it serves as a canvas on which we can form a clearer picture of our thoughts, motivations, and actions. Writing in a journal can be particularly powerful because it externalises our internal dialogues, giving us distance to scrutinise beliefs and behaviours with a more objective lens.

The Power of Becoming

In this space of vulnerability, we can ask probing questions: What patterns do I notice in my decision-making? How do I respond to criticism? What assumptions do I hold that may limit my relationships or growth? The answers may not come easily, but the pursuit is worthwhile. The act of writing creates clarity, helping us locate blind spots that might otherwise remain concealed in the chaos of our thoughts. It also fosters a deeper understanding of our motivations and emotional responses. Recognising why we react in certain ways, or identifying which triggers elicit strong reactions, can provide significant insight into blind spots. The key is to confront these facets of ourselves with kindness and honesty, recognising that this process is integral to our journey of self-discovery and growth.

While self-reflection is essential, relying solely on our internal lens can be limiting. This is where soliciting feedback from others becomes invaluable. Often, the people close to us—friends, family, colleagues—can see aspects of our behaviour that we overlook. Their perspectives can serve as catalysts for breakthroughs, offering a clearer view of our blind spots. Seeking feedback requires courage; it invites the potential for criticism, and that vulnerability can be uncomfortable. Yet, when we approach feedback as a tool for growth rather than a threat, we can harness its power to foster deeper understanding.

To solicit feedback effectively, create the right environment. Establish trust with those you approach so they feel safe sharing observations without fear of repercussions. Express your desire for honest and constructive insights, and be clear about the areas you would like to explore. Perhaps you want to know how others perceive your listening skills or whether you come across as approachable. When the feedback comes, practise active listening.

Resist the urge to defend yourself or dismiss observations. Instead, take note, reflect, and consider how this information fits into your self-awareness journey.

Consider Sarah, a project manager who took pride in her leadership abilities. She was well-liked and received positive reviews. However, during a routine feedback session, her team expressed concerns that she often dominated meetings, making it difficult for others to share their ideas. Initially defensive, Sarah dismissed the feedback. On reflection, she recognised a pattern. With the help of a mentor, she re-evaluated her communication style and implemented practices to encourage participation. By acknowledging her blind spot, she transformed her leadership and fostered a more inclusive team environment.

As we grapple with the discomfort of our blind spots, it helps to remember the growth that follows. Each uncomfortable revelation is an opportunity to expand our understanding of ourselves and our impact on others. Embracing these lessons cultivates resilience and adaptability, empowering us to navigate our journeys with greater ease.

Finding a mentor or accountability partner is another valuable way to identify and address blind spots. These individuals offer valuable insights from their experiences and perspectives, illuminating areas that we may not have noticed. Sharing goals and challenges with someone who has our best interests at heart enhances self-awareness. A mentor may ask questions we hadn't considered or provide feedback that shifts our perspective.

Structured tools and assessments can complement reflection and interpersonal feedback. Personality profiles or 360-degree processes can illuminate strengths and blind spots, providing context for our behaviour and thought patterns. They help pinpoint areas for growth that may have remained hidden.

When confronting blind spots, it is essential to consider one's own biases. Unconscious biases are ingrained attitudes or stereotypes that influence our understanding, actions, and decisions without our awareness. They can influence how we perceive others and ourselves, sometimes leading to distorted judgements. Being cognisant of biases—whether related to race, gender, age, or other aspects—can reveal where we need to grow in empathy and understanding. Conversations about diversity and inclusion can challenge biases and broaden perspectives.

Real-life anecdotes further highlight the value of acknowledging blind spots. James, a successful entrepreneur, sought a business coach during a period of stagnation. He unearthed a blind spot: reluctance to delegate. Proud of being hands-on, he was unintentionally hampering growth. By recognising this and empowering his team, he improved operations and morale while freeing himself for strategic work.

Similarly, Anna initially resisted colleagues' feedback, believing she understood her role clearly. Through a team exercise encouraging open dialogue, she confronted her tendency to dominate discussions. She committed to inviting others in, which strengthened relationships and made her a more effective collaborator.

In pursuing our best selves, we must embrace the discomfort that accompanies acknowledging blind spots. This requires vulnerability and a willingness to listen, but the rewards are profound. By illuminating hidden biases, habits, and perceptions, we pave the way for genuine growth and transformation. Embracing blind spots is not self-criticism; it is opening ourselves to the possibilities of who we can become.

As you conclude this section, reflect on blind spots in your life. Reflect on the habits or beliefs that may be holding you back and consider how you can engage with others to uncover hidden barriers. Embrace feedback as a gift rather than a criticism, and recognise that every discovery, while potentially uncomfortable, is a stepping stone on your journey towards your best self. Growth is a process, and every step towards deeper understanding contributes to the remarkable journey of becoming.

Mindset Matters

Understanding Fixed vs. Growth Mindset

Mindset significantly influences not only how we think but also how we approach life and pursue ambitions. At the heart of this is the distinction between two fundamental mindsets: fixed and growth. Coined and popularised by psychologist Carol Dweck, these terms encapsulate attitudes towards learning, intelligence, and development. Understanding them is essential for anyone on a journey of growth, as they frame our perceptions and behaviours in ways that can either propel us forward or hold us back.

A fixed mindset is characterised by the belief that abilities, intelligence, and talents are static traits. Individuals with a fixed mindset often see qualities as predetermined. They may avoid challenges, give up readily when setbacks occur, and view effort as fruitless. They can feel threatened by others' success, which seems to undermine their sense of ability. This mindset limits growth and fosters a fear of failure because mistakes appear to expose a lack of innate competence.

By contrast, a growth mindset is rooted in the belief that abilities can be developed through dedication, practice, and perseverance. Those who adopt it see challenges as opportunities to learn. They embrace effort as a path to mastery and show resilience in the face of setbacks. Rather than feeling threatened by others' success, they find inspiration and are often motivated by peers' achievements. They are more willing to take measured risks beyond their comfort zone, understanding that failure is part of learning.

The Power of Becoming

Dweck's research, conducted over many years with students of varying ages, showed that those who believed their abilities could be developed tended to achieve higher levels of success than peers who believed abilities were fixed. In one well-known study, after a series of increasingly difficult puzzles, growth-minded students expressed excitement about learning new strategies. In contrast, fixed-minded students showed frustration and a desire to give up. These findings underscore the significant impact of mindset on performance across various domains, including education, work, sports, and relationships.

Relatable scenarios make the distinction tangible. A student who receives a poor mark in maths might, with a fixed mindset, think, 'I'm not good at maths,' and avoid further study. With a growth mindset, they would think, 'I need to adjust how I study and seek help,' and approach the next test with renewed determination.

In the workplace, an employee receiving critical feedback may react differently depending on their mindset. With a fixed mindset, feedback can feel like a personal indictment: 'My skills are inadequate.' With a growth mindset, feedback is information: 'This shows how I can improve.' The latter response drives learning, satisfaction, and advancement.

The contrast extends to relationships. Faced with a difficult conversation, someone with a fixed mindset may avoid it, fearing they will say the wrong thing and damage the relationship. A growth-minded person leans into the challenge, viewing it as an opportunity to strengthen their connection, approaching it with curiosity and listening carefully.

Adopting a growth mindset also has wider implications. In education, valuing effort and strategy over supposed innate ability fosters richer learning. In organisations, cultures that normalise experimentation and learning from failure are more innovative and adaptive. Leaders who model a growth mindset inspire teams to face challenges with resilience.

Cultivating a growth mindset is not mere positive thinking. It requires genuine engagement with learning and a willingness to experience discomfort. It may mean challenging long-held beliefs about our capabilities and acknowledging insecurities. Recognising that learning is lifelong and that everyone makes mistakes is fundamental.

Practical steps help embed this mindset:

- **Shift language:** replace 'I can't do this' with 'I can't do this yet.'

- **Recall evidence:** reflect on times when effort led to improvement to reinforce belief in growth.

- **Set incremental goals:** focus on small, achievable steps and celebrate progress.

- **Reframe mistakes:** treat setbacks as information rather than verdicts.

- **Choose your company:** spend time with people who model and encourage learning, resilience, and constructive feedback.

In summary, understanding fixed and growth mindsets is critical for anyone seeking to become their best self. Dweck's insights provide a framework for recognising how beliefs about ability shape our reality. By adopting a growth mindset, we cultivate resilience, deepen engagement in learning, and open ourselves to broader possibilities.

Growth is not a destination but an ongoing process. Choosing a growth mindset invites transformation at the personal level and within our relationships and communities. It invites us to see ourselves not only as we are but as we may become. In doing so, we step firmly onto the path of becoming—an enduring journey towards our best selves.

Cultivating Resilience Through Cognitive Shifts

The journey of resilience often begins with how we perceive failures and challenges. Rather than viewing them as insurmountable obstacles, reframing negative experiences as opportunities for growth is essential. This shift not only alters our emotional response but also equips us with tools to navigate life's difficulties more effectively. In this section, we explore techniques that facilitate this cognitive shift and share brief stories that highlight the transformative power of resilience.

Understanding resilience starts with recognising its significance in our lives. When we face setbacks—whether personal disappointments, professional failures, or unexpected life changes—our natural inclination may be to give in to despair or frustration. However, cultivating resilience allows us to bounce back and adapt, providing a pathway to both emotional and mental strength. The critical question then becomes: how do we shift our mindset to foster such resilience?

First and foremost, embracing a growth mindset, as advocated by Carol Dweck, is fundamental. A growth mindset is predicated on the belief that our abilities and intelligence can be developed over time. This belief turns failures into stepping stones rather than stopping points. By adopting this perspective, we begin to view challenges as opportunities for learning. For instance, instead of thinking, 'I failed at this task; I'll never succeed,' we might reframe it to, 'This setback is a chance for me to learn and grow.' This shift in thinking lays the groundwork for resilience.

Next, consider cognitive reframing. This psychological approach involves viewing a situation from a different perspective to change its emotional impact. For example, if we experience a job loss, rather than perceiving it solely as failure, we can reframe it as a fresh opportunity to pursue our passions or explore new career avenues. To practise cognitive reframing, ask: 'What can I learn from this experience?' or 'How can this setback lead me to something better?' These questions encourage a focus on potential rather than negativity, bolstering resilience.

Affirmations can also play a role in reshaping one's mindset. Affirmations are positive statements that help challenge and overcome self-sabotaging thoughts. By regularly repeating statements that promote resilience, we reinforce belief in our ability to face challenges. Examples include: 'I am capable of overcoming my struggles' and 'Every setback is an opportunity for growth.' Integrating such affirmations into daily routines can shift outlook and strengthen mental resilience over time.

Another practical strategy involves setting realistic and attainable goals. When faced with a significant setback, the bigger picture can feel overwhelming. Breaking objectives into smaller, manageable tasks creates a sense of progress and achievement. Each small victory reduces feelings of helplessness and reinforces our capacity to navigate challenges, thereby improving our overall resilience.

Consider Jay, a young entrepreneur whose start-up abruptly collapsed. Rather than succumbing to despair, he adopted a growth mindset, sought feedback, and identified gaps in his approach. By reframing failure as a learning experience, he pivoted and launched a second venture aligned with his passions. His resilience turned a devastating setback into a launchpad, inspiring others in his community.

Building resilience also involves embracing challenges rather than avoiding them. Willingness to step outside our comfort zones is a key indicator of potential growth. For instance, someone with public-speaking anxiety might begin by sharing thoughts in small groups, gradually progressing to larger audiences. Each experience, whatever the outcome, fosters resilience and confidence.

We can draw further motivation from Maya, who confronted life-altering health challenges. Facing chronic illness, she adopted a proactive approach: attending support groups, engaging with others in similar situations, and advocating for herself. She celebrated small victories—completing a daily walk, managing symptoms, and finding joy in little things. Her journey exemplifies the connection between resilience and the willingness to confront life's inherent challenges.

To deepen resilience, cultivate an attitude of gratitude. Research consistently shows that practising gratitude can improve mental well-being and resilience. Focusing on what we are thankful for, even in the face of adversity, creates a psychological buffer against stressors. Keeping a gratitude journal—recording small wins and moments of joy—can shift attention away from negativity and foster a mindset that emphasises abundance and growth.

Mindfulness is another effective tool. It cultivates awareness and acceptance of thoughts and feelings without judgement, creating space between experience and reaction. When difficulties arise, mindfulness helps us pause and respond rather than react impulsively. Techniques such as meditation, deep breathing, and grounding exercises enable us to remain centred, turning potentially detrimental thoughts into constructive reflections.

David, a businessman facing financial ruin during a market downturn, turned to mindfulness to regain control. Through meditation and reflective practice, he gained a clearer understanding of his emotional responses and the situation. This clarity enabled him to make informed decisions that eventually turned his business around, illustrating how mindfulness can support resilient thinking.

A crucial aspect of building resilience is having a strong support network. Relationships have a significant impact on our ability to cope with adversity. Cultivating connections with people who encourage us, offer honest feedback, and uplift us creates a support structure that enhances resilience. Linda, experiencing a major life transition, initially isolated herself. Re-engaging with friends and family provided the encouragement and perspective she needed, helping her reframe challenges and draw strength from connection.

It is also worth noting that humour can help. Embracing laughter amid adversity can create lightness that facilitates coping. People who find humour in difficult situations often develop a perspective that helps them navigate tough situations with greater ease.

In conclusion, cultivating resilience through cognitive shifts is a practical pathway to transforming our approach to challenges and failures. Techniques such as adopting a growth mindset, practising cognitive reframing, gratitude, mindfulness, and setting manageable goals can enhance our ability to rebound from adversity. The stories above illustrate that resilience is within reach. By applying these strategies, we strengthen emotional resources and empower ourselves on the path to becoming our best selves. The journey towards resilience is ongoing, shaped by experience and by our willingness to meet it with courage and determination.

The Role of Affirmations

Affirmations are powerful declarations that can shape beliefs and influence personal narratives. They express what we aspire to be and reinforce positive states of mind. At their core, affirmations bridge the gap between where we are today and where we envision ourselves in the future. Their transformative power lies in their ability to influence the subconscious, helping us break free from limitations imposed by negative self-talk and ingrained beliefs.

Understanding the effectiveness of affirmations involves recognising the relationship between thoughts, beliefs, and behaviours. Psychologists have long noted that subconscious beliefs shape how we perceive the world and navigate our lives. Negative judgments about ourselves may be deeply ingrained, having been absorbed through years of conditioning and experience. Yet, as negative beliefs can be formed, they can also be dismantled and replaced with empowering alternatives through the strategic use of positive affirmations.

Personalised affirmations act as a counter-narrative, challenging self-doubt and perceived inadequacy. To create effective affirmations, ensure they resonate with your aspirations. Begin by identifying areas where you seek growth or change, such as confidence, career progress, relationships, or overall well-being. Ask open-ended questions to uncover the beliefs that may be limiting progress. If you aspire to be more confident but feel shy in social settings, consider the beliefs that contribute to that feeling. Perhaps you believe others will not accept you or that your voice is not worth hearing. Reframe each limiting belief with a corresponding affirmation. Instead of 'I am not good enough,' try 'I am worthy of love and respect.'

You can also incorporate specific qualities you wish to embody. For example, 'I embrace my ability to learn and grow from every experience' fosters a growth mindset while emphasising resilience and adaptability—qualities essential on the journey of becoming.

With a crafted set of affirmations, integrate them into your daily routine. Consistency is key. Choose times you can dedicate to affirmations. Morning rituals are potent: on waking, before distractions begin, recite your affirmations and visualise yourself embodying them throughout the day. You can also pair affirmations with physical activity, such as during a walk or a workout, reinforcing them through movement. Place affirmations in visible spaces—such as mirrors, desks, or phone reminders—to keep them at the forefront of your mind.

The Power of Becoming

The science behind affirmations helps explain their impact. Research suggests that affirmations can activate reward pathways in the brain, promote positive feelings, and strengthen belief in our capacity for change. Engaging with affirmations can also help reduce stress and enhance overall well-being. Studies on neuroplasticity indicate that the brain can reorganise itself through thought and experience, so repeated affirmations can help create new neural pathways, gradually shifting habitual thinking patterns about self-worth and capability.

Acknowledge the emotions tied to your affirmations. Simply repeating words without genuine belief limits effectiveness. For affirmations to resonate, infuse them with authentic feeling. When speaking your affirmation, allow yourself to experience the associated emotion. You might visualise a past success or a moment of joy while affirming, anchoring the words to a positive experience.

Remain flexible. Your journey is dynamic, and your affirmations should evolve with your goals. Check in regularly and adjust your statements to ensure they remain relevant and aligned with your development. Practise patience. Deeply rooted beliefs do not shift overnight. Commit to the process and celebrate small wins. Over time, integrating affirmations into daily life contributes to a more positive self-image and a greater sense of agency.

In conclusion, affirmations are an invaluable tool on the journey to becoming your best self. By reshaping beliefs and fostering a constructive mindset, they open the door to growth and self-discovery. Craft personalised affirmations that resonate with your aspirations, integrate them consistently, and let the practice evolve with you. Becoming is a step-by-step process—affirmation by affirmation. Let the power of words support and propel you on your path.

The Power of Habits

Building Keystone Habits

Habits shape our lives in profound ways, often without our conscious realisation. They are the routines and behaviours that form our daily existence, playing a crucial role in how we perform tasks, make decisions, and interact with the world around us. Among the thousands of habits we can cultivate, some carry greater weight than others. These are known as keystone habits.

This subchapter explores the concept of keystone habits, their transformative power, and how they can be instrumental in initiating significant change across various aspects of our lives.

At their core, habits are automatic responses cultivated through repetition. When we engage in a behaviour repeatedly, it becomes embedded in our neural pathways, making it less dependent on conscious decision-making. This automation frees up mental energy for more complex tasks, allowing us to lead more efficient lives. While many everyday habits may seem benign or small, keystone habits can set off a chain reaction of transformation, influencing our behaviours, attitudes, and even our relationships.

The term 'keystone habit' was popularised by Charles Duhigg in his book The Power of Habit. Duhigg described these habits as foundational ones that, when adopted, can create ripple effects leading to positive changes in other behaviours and areas of life. For example, regular exercise is often cited as a keystone habit because it can lead to improved eating choices, better sleep patterns, increased productivity, and enhanced self-esteem. By focusing on a single keystone habit, individuals can catalyse widespread improvements in their overall quality of life.

Research suggests that certain habits have a particularly significant impact. A study conducted by researchers at the University of Pennsylvania found that certain lifestyle changes, such as adopting a consistent exercise routine, had a positive influence on other domains of participants' lives. Those who exercised regularly reported improved eating habits, better mood, increased focus, and greater engagement in social activities. This interconnectedness implies that by targeting keystone habits, individuals can initiate a cascade of positive changes that align with their goals for becoming their best selves.

Identifying keystone habits requires a thoughtful approach. Here are some practical steps to help you pinpoint which habits might serve as the cornerstone of your transformation:

1. Reflect on Your Life Goals: Start by identifying the primary goals you wish to achieve in your life. Consider all dimensions—physical, emotional, social, and professional. What areas feel stagnant or unfulfilled? Understanding your aspirations will provide clarity on the kinds of transformations you seek.
2. Analyse Your Current Patterns: Take stock of your daily routines and behaviours. What habits do you currently possess? How do they contribute to or detract from your goals? Keep a journal for a week, noting your habits and reflecting on their impacts. This self-assessment will help you identify which current habits are not serving you and which ones hold potential.

3. Consider the Ripple Effects: When evaluating potential keystone habits, think about how one habit may influence others. For instance, would adopting a daily habit of mindfulness meditation encourage you to be more present in your relationships? Would starting a gratitude journal prompt you to focus more on positivity in your life? Look for habits that have the potential to extend their benefits beyond their immediate context.
4. Start Small: When establishing a new keystone habit, approach it gradually. The power of small wins cannot be underestimated: accomplishing a minor goal can help build momentum and confidence. If you choose to pursue regular exercise as a keystone habit, begin with a simple daily walk rather than an intense workout regimen that feels overwhelming. The key is to make the habit sustainable and enjoyable.
5. Create Visual Reminders: To reinforce your commitment to your keystone habits, create visual cues that serve as reminders in your environment. Sticky notes, calendar alerts, or vision boards can help you stay focused on your goals. These reminders can act as prompts that trigger the desired behaviour, making it easier to stay the course.
6. Track Your Progress: Harness the power of tracking to maintain motivation and accountability. Keep a record of your commitment to your keystone habits and the changes you notice in other areas of your life. This exercise will not only reinforce your dedication but also help you appreciate the transformations that result from your efforts.
7. Be Patient and Adaptable: Change does not happen overnight. Allow yourself the grace to stumble and learn from the challenges that come your way. If you find that a

chosen keystone habit is not producing the desired effects, reflect on why that may be and adapt your approach. Remaining flexible in your commitment is essential for long-term success.
8. Involve Others: Share your keystone habit journey with friends or family who can act as your support system. Having accountability partners can increase your motivation and make the process more enjoyable. Perhaps consider group activities such as joining a fitness class or a book club centred around personal development.

Different keystone habits will uniquely resonate with each individual, aligning with their personal values and goals. Here are a few examples of keystone habits that have demonstrated significant impact:

- Regular Exercise: Integrating consistent physical activity into your weekly routine can lead not only to health benefits but also to improved mental clarity, increased energy levels, and enhanced willpower over time.
- Mindfulness Practices: Engaging in mindfulness meditation can shift your perspective and emotional responses to daily challenges. Individuals who practise mindfulness often report greater emotional resilience, improved focus, and stronger relationships.
- Structured Meal Planning: Taking the time to plan and prepare meals can encourage healthier eating habits and foster a greater awareness of food choices. This habit may lead to reduced food waste, better nutrition, and a more intimate relationship with personal health.
- Daily Journaling: The act of journaling enables reflection and fosters self-awareness. People who regularly jot down

their thoughts often find clarity on their motivations and desires, fostering a deeper understanding of themselves and their journeys.
- Consistent Sleep Routines: Establishing a regular sleep schedule can accelerate improvements in mood, energy, and cognitive functionality, creating positive feedback loops that enable fuller engagement in other habits.

As you consider the concept of keystone habits, it is important to recognise that they do not exist in isolation. They are influenced by the interplay of our environment, social circles, and mental states. To achieve lasting transformation, we must also consider the systems that surround us. Analyse how your immediate environment supports or hinders your keystone habits. A supportive environment may include decluttering your workspace to enhance productivity or choosing healthier food options that are readily available at home.

In addition, keystone habits are often closely tied to our identity. As we cultivate these habits, they contribute to our self-concept, reinforcing our beliefs about who we are and who we aspire to be. Embracing a keystone habit can lead to a shift in identity; for instance, adopting a running habit may transform your self-perception from 'I dislike exercise' to 'I am an active person'. This shift can catalyse further behavioural changes, aligning your actions with your evolving identity.

As you embark on your journey to establish keystone habits, approach the process with curiosity and self-compassion. Realise that becoming your best self is a dynamic endeavour. Embrace the twists and turns along the way. Allow the keystone habits you choose to become a source of joy, discovery, and growth. Celebrate each bit of progress, however small, as it is part of your unique path of becoming.

In conclusion, the concept of keystone habits provides a powerful framework for understanding how specific behaviours can foster widespread change in our lives. By recognising the profound impact these habits have, we can take intentional steps to cultivate those that resonate with our goals and values. Remember, the journey of becoming our best selves is not solely about achieving specific outcomes but about the depth of growth, self-awareness, and resilience that accompany that journey. Through the intentional establishment of keystone habits, we empower ourselves to unlock transformative potential and create the life we envision.

Creating Effective Rituals

Rituals and routines often serve as the backbone of our daily lives, acting as anchors that keep us grounded amidst the chaos and unpredictability of existence. Through the lens of habit formation, effective rituals become a crucial element in our journey towards becoming our best selves.

In this subchapter, we explore the importance of building effective rituals, how they can enhance habit formation, and how to create rituals that resonate deeply with our personal values and lifestyles.

Effective rituals do not simply exist in isolation; they are woven into the fabric of our day-to-day experiences, creating a sense of purpose that helps us stay aligned with our goals. These rituals can be as straightforward as a morning cup of tea that centres our thoughts or as complex as a multi-step evening routine designed to wind down and reflect on the day's achievements. The beauty of rituals lies in their intentionality—the deliberate choice to engage in an activity that reflects our values, priorities, and aspirations.

To embark upon the path of creating effective rituals, begin by examining your existing routines. Reflect on what rituals, if any, you currently practise. At what times do you feel most in alignment with your values? Where do you notice resistance or a lack of motivation? These reflections serve as a compass, guiding you towards understanding what works and what does not in your life. Once you take stock of your current habits, the next step is to craft rituals that resonate deeply and serve as powerful tools for habit formation.

The first principle of creating effective rituals is clarity of purpose. A well-defined purpose allows you to align your actions with your ultimate goals. For example, if your goal is to cultivate mindfulness, a morning meditation ritual may be a suitable choice. Conversely, if you aim to enhance productivity at work, starting the day with a clear to-do list can serve as a practical ritual that sets the tone for success. By identifying the outcomes you desire, you can tailor rituals that directly support your intentions.

Equally important is the idea of consistency. Effective rituals should be easy to integrate into your daily life. This does not mean they must be monotonous; rather, they should evolve while maintaining their core purpose. Begin by selecting rituals that require minimal effort but yield substantial returns. For example, setting aside just five minutes each day to journal can significantly enhance self-awareness and reflection over time, even if the ritual seems small initially. As you gain traction and experience the benefits, you may find yourself naturally expanding and enriching them.

The Power of Becoming

To help provide a foundation for your ritual creation, it may be useful to consider templates or frameworks that you can adapt to your preferences.

- The Daily Check-In: This straightforward practice encourages mindfulness and reflection. Each morning or evening, dedicate a few minutes to asking yourself key questions: How am I feeling today? What do I want to achieve? What aspects of my life am I grateful for at this moment? This simple practice not only grounds you in the moment but also fosters a greater sense of self-awareness over time.
- Intention Setting: Each week, dedicate time to reflecting on your intentions for the upcoming days. This ritual can take place on a Sunday evening, allowing you to envision and map out your goals. Setting intentions acts as a guiding star throughout the week, helping you remain focused on your priorities. Write them down and display them somewhere visible to reinforce your commitment.
- Gratitude Rituals: Engaging in gratitude practices, whether through journaling or expressing appreciation to others, has a profound impact on mental and emotional well-being. Create a ritual of gratitude by dedicating a specific time each day to express appreciation. This simple yet meaningful practice can foster a positive mindset that impacts every aspect of your life.

When creating rituals, it is essential to ensure these practices align with your core values and lifestyle. Rituals should resonate with you personally, enhancing your engagement and desire to maintain them. Choose activities that evoke joy, curiosity, or mindfulness. For example, if connecting with nature is vital to your

The Power of Becoming

well-being, consider crafting a ritual that incorporates time outdoors—whether through a morning walk, gardening, or simply sitting in a park. When your rituals reflect what matters most to you, they become natural extensions of your identity rather than obligations.

It is also important to remain adaptable. Life is not static, and the circumstances that surround us can shift. Your rituals should evolve in tandem with your growth and life changes. If a particular ritual begins to feel obligatory rather than fulfilling, reassess and make adjustments. The goal is engagement, not adherence for its own sake.

Additionally, incorporating elements of symbolic action can enhance the emotional resonance of your rituals. Symbols can strengthen the connection between intention and practice. For instance, if you are starting a new exercise routine, create a dedicated space in your home for fitness. Visual reminders or objects that represent your goals—such as a yoga mat, weights, or a reading corner—can deepen your commitment to your rituals.

Accountability is another key component. Share your intentions with a trusted friend or join a community that supports similar goals. Having others involved can increase motivation and strengthen your resolve. Consider forming a buddy system to check in on progress, share insights, and encourage one another along the journey.

Finally, remember to celebrate small wins. Acknowledge your progress, however modest it may seem. Reflecting on what you have achieved reinforces positive behaviour and keeps you motivated. Each step forward is a testament to your growth and a reminder of your ability to transform.

As you embark on your journey towards creating effective rituals, remember that perfection is not the goal. Focus on creating meaningful experiences that align with your values, empower your habits, and foster a connection with your authentic self. Rituals are not only about achieving an end goal; they are about enhancing the everyday experience of living, ultimately leading to a more purposeful existence.

In conclusion, rituals are powerful allies in the quest for habit formation and personal growth. By understanding the importance of clarity, consistency, and adaptability, you can craft rituals that resonate with your life's values and aspirations. Use the frameworks and examples provided to develop your own effective rituals that pave the way towards becoming your best self. With intention and commitment, the rituals you create can anchor your goals, enrich your life, and illuminate the path towards the person you aspire to be.

Staying Committed: Overcoming Resistance

Staying committed to new habits can often feel like navigating a labyrinth. Each turn may present obstacles, distractions, fears, and self-doubt that threaten to derail our best intentions. Understanding and overcoming these forms of resistance is crucial for lasting change. This section examines the common challenges individuals encounter during habit formation, along with effective strategies for managing procrastination, promoting accountability, and ultimately sustaining commitment to personal growth.

One of the most prevalent forms of resistance is procrastination. We all know the feeling—perhaps it is the draining weight of a task that seems uninviting, or the alluring pull of something less demanding. Procrastination can become a familiar companion on the journey of habit formation, often masquerading as a rational decision to delay the inevitable. Recognising procrastination for what it is—a barrier to progress—is the first step towards overcoming it.

Understanding why we procrastinate is crucial. Researchers have identified several underlying causes, including fear of failure, perfectionism, and a lack of motivation. Fear of failure, for instance, can lead us to avoid starting a task altogether rather than risk falling short of our goals. This kind of avoidance is deeply rooted in our psyche and can be debilitating. Furthermore, perfectionism can cause us to delay action in favour of flawless execution that may never come. These emotional roadblocks create fertile ground for procrastination to flourish, becoming a major barrier to habit formation.

The first step in overcoming procrastination is to identify and address these fears. Journalling can be a powerful tool in this regard. By writing down the specific fears and thoughts that surface when faced with a new habit, you can visualise the barriers blocking your path. What is it that you fear? How would it feel to confront that fear? Once we acknowledge these thoughts, we can challenge and reframe them. If perfectionism is a factor, it is important to remind ourselves that progress outweighs perfection. Setting realistic standards instead of unattainable ideals can help alleviate the pressure that leads to procrastination.

Another effective strategy to combat procrastination is to break tasks into smaller, more manageable parts. Large goals can feel overwhelming and unachievable, but dissecting them into bite-sized tasks reduces the intimidation factor. For example, if you aim to read a book each month, begin by setting a goal to read just one chapter a day. This smaller approach turns a daunting commitment into a simple daily habit, making the process feel less burdensome. Establishing a routine around these small tasks can create a sense of accomplishment, further fuelling commitment.

Additionally, time-blocking can serve as an effective technique for allocating specific periods to habit practice. By scheduling uninterrupted time for your new habit within your daily routine, you actively reduce distractions and establish boundaries between your goals and the noise of daily life. For instance, if you are working towards a fitness goal, carve out a dedicated time each day solely for exercise. Treat this time as a crucial appointment that should not be missed.

Alongside procrastination, another barrier to habit formation lies in a lack of accountability. When we embark on a journey of personal growth, it can be tempting to let ourselves off the hook. Without external accountability measures, we might find it easier to abandon our habits at the first sign of difficulty. Having a support system in place can significantly bolster commitment.

One effective strategy to enhance accountability is to share your goals with others. Whether it is friends, family, or support groups, vocalising your intentions creates a sense of responsibility. You are more likely to stick to your habits when others are aware of your ambitions. Imagine telling a friend that you aim to meditate daily. Knowing that they might ask about your progress can motivate you to stay consistent. Alternatively, find an accountability partner—someone who shares similar goals and is willing to check in regularly. This mutual support creates a system of reinforcement where both parties can encourage each other through obstacles. It is a reminder that you are not alone in your struggle; you have someone beside you who understands and can inspire you to keep moving forward.

Technology can also play a pivotal role in accountability. Numerous apps and online platforms are designed to help users track their habits and progress. For instance, habit-tracking applications send reminders and allow you to visualise your achievements over time. Seeing your progress, no matter how small, can be incredibly motivating. Additionally, many platforms allow for social sharing, enabling you to connect with others at various stages of forming a habit.

While accountability is fundamental, embracing a shift in perspective regarding setbacks is equally important. Instead of viewing mistakes as failures, consider them learning opportunities—chances for growth and improvement. When you stumble or fall short of your goals, reflect on the experience, analyse what led to the setback, and embrace the lessons it offers. This mindset can transform discomfort into fuel for resilience.

In many lives, the power of storytelling plays a vital role. Hearing the experiences of others who have successfully navigated barriers of resistance can serve as both inspiration and motivation. Consider the story of Anna, who struggled to maintain her commitment to a healthy lifestyle. Initially filled with enthusiasm, she soon found herself overwhelmed by everyday responsibilities and self-doubt. At one point, she realised her initial goal was too grand; instead, she needed smaller, achievable objectives. By starting with ten-minute workout videos, she gradually built her stamina. Each small victory reinforced her motivation, and she eventually found herself exercising for longer periods of time. By sharing her journey on social media, she not only kept herself accountable but also inspired countless others to embark on their own paths to health.

Similarly, there is the story of David, who aspired to write a novel but found himself constantly distracted by the bustle of daily life. Rather than abandoning his goal, he chose to write one page a day. This small commitment felt achievable within his busy schedule and, over time, it grew into chapters, eventually culminating in a completed manuscript. Sharing his progress with his writing group, he found support among fellow writers who were on similar journeys. His success invigorated his commitment and encouraged others to persist through their struggles.

These narratives exemplify the human spirit's resilience. They remind us that everyone faces obstacles, yet those who succeed do so by learning to navigate resistance creatively. Each individual's journey provides valuable lessons, showing that our struggles are part of the larger tapestry of growth.

Another angle to consider in overcoming resistance is the concept of creating a habit stack. This technique, introduced by James Clear in his book Atomic Habits, encourages individuals to anchor new habits onto existing ones. By stacking a desired habit onto a well-established routine, you create an automatic cue that signals the time to act. For example, if you consistently brew your morning coffee, consider adding a short meditation while it percolates. This connection makes the new habit more likely to stick.

Moreover, visualisation can also play a pivotal role in staying committed. Envisioning your future self—who you will become once your new habits are ingrained—can provide clarity and motivation. Imagine what success looks like for you; picture yourself achieving your goal, experiencing joy and fulfilment in that state. This mental imagery can serve as a powerful reminder on tough days, reigniting your desire to overcome resistance.

Additionally, the role of positive reinforcement cannot be underestimated. Celebrating small victories fosters a rewarding sense of progress. Whether it is treating yourself to something you enjoy, acknowledging your efforts, or sharing your successes with others, recognising achievements motivates you to keep striving forward. Create milestones in your journey, and when you reach them, take a moment to reflect on the effort it took to achieve them. Reward yourself not just for the outcome but for the commitment shown along the way.

In conclusion, forming new habits is a journey filled with challenges, yet it is also rich in opportunities for growth and self-discovery. Resistance manifests in many forms, with procrastination, lack of accountability, and fear of failure standing out as the most common obstacles. However, by acknowledging these barriers, employing strategic tools, and learning from the experiences of others, we can cultivate the resilience required to overcome them.

Remember that every small commitment adds up to monumental change. Stay focused on the journey while being kind to yourself during setbacks. Embrace the concept of lifelong evolution—each new habit you adopt paves the way for a better version of yourself. As you harness the strategies discussed in this subchapter, may you find the strength to transcend resistance and emerge more committed than ever on your path towards becoming your best self.

Emotional Mastery

Understanding Your Emotions

Emotions are an integral part of the human experience. They colour our perceptions, influence our decisions, and shape our interactions with others. Yet many of us go through life without fully understanding the emotions we feel or recognising their impact on our day-to-day existence.

In this subchapter, we explore the vast spectrum of human emotions, the concept of emotional intelligence, and the techniques that allow for effective recognition and labelling of our feelings. By doing so, we pave the way for deeper emotional mastery that lays the foundation for personal growth and transformation.

To begin, it is essential to acknowledge the complexity of emotions. They can be categorised into primary and secondary feelings. Primary emotions include joy, sadness, fear, anger, surprise, and disgust. These are the most fundamental and universally understood concepts across cultures. They arise instinctively in response to stimuli from our environment—situations, events, or even memories. Secondary emotions, on the other hand, are more nuanced. They arise from our interpretations and thoughts about primary emotions. For instance, feeling shame after expressing anger or guilt following a moment of joy exemplifies how secondary emotions can complicate our emotional landscape.

Understanding emotions requires recognising their transient nature. They are ephemeral by essence, often fluctuating within moments. The practice of being present with one's emotions rather than reacting impulsively is a critical skill. This mindfulness encourages us to observe our feelings without immediate judgement, allowing for deeper insights into their origins and effects. However inconvenient they may be, our emotions reveal something vital about our needs and boundaries. Reflecting on the triggers of our emotions is, therefore, beneficial for personal development.

Emotional intelligence, or EQ, is the ability to recognise, understand, and manage our emotions, as well as those of others. Developed by psychologists Peter Salovey and John D. Mayer, and later popularised by Daniel Goleman, emotional intelligence encompasses several components: self-awareness, self-regulation, motivation, empathy, and social skills. High emotional intelligence is associated with better mental health, improved relationships, enhanced leadership abilities, and greater overall life satisfaction.

Self-awareness, the first component of emotional intelligence, refers to recognising one's own emotional state. It entails understanding the internal signals that indicate when we are experiencing different emotions. Journalling serves as an excellent tool for cultivating self-awareness. By regularly writing about daily experiences and the emotions they evoke, we create a map of our emotional landscape. Reviewing these entries reveals patterns that illuminate how certain triggers consistently elicit specific feelings, leading to greater insight about ourselves.

Self-regulation, the second element, involves managing our emotions effectively. Once we recognise our emotions, the challenge lies in responding to them constructively. This does not mean suppressing them—that only leads to pent-up frustration—but finding ways to express them appropriately and channelling them into positive action. For example, when feeling anger, one might engage in physical activity, practise relaxation techniques, or have a constructive conversation with the source of frustration rather than reacting explosively. This thoughtful approach allows us to navigate emotional turbulence without compromising well-being or relationships.

Motivation, the third aspect of emotional intelligence, refers to the internal drive that inspires us to pursue goals and remain resilient in the face of setbacks. Emotions play a crucial role in motivation. When we feel passionate about something, our emotional investment enhances commitment and determination. Conversely, negative emotions such as fear or self-doubt can hinder progress. Recognising these emotions allows us to reframe them—transforming fear into motivation, for instance, igniting a drive to learn and improve. The ability to persist, even in the face of adversity, is a hallmark of emotional mastery.

Empathy, the fourth component, is the ability to understand and share the feelings of others. It is a vital skill for building strong relationships and fostering deeper connections. By becoming attuned to the emotional states of those around us, we can respond with compassion and support. Practising active listening—fully concentrating, understanding, responding, and remembering what is being said—significantly enhances empathic ability. Such interactions build trust and open communication, creating supportive environments where emotional nuances can be explored freely.

Social skills, the final element, encompass the abilities required to manage relationships and navigate social complexities. Effective communication, conflict resolution, and collaboration all arise from well-developed social skills. Recognising our emotions and those of others facilitates better interactions, leading to stronger networks of support. The ability to express oneself clearly while considering emotional tone is crucial in both personal and professional settings.

To harness the power of emotional mastery, we must first develop the skills of recognising and labelling emotions effectively. Begin with emotional check-ins throughout the day. Set aside moments to pause and assess how you feel—physically and emotionally. Acknowledge the sensations within your body: Are your shoulders tense, and is your heart racing? These physical cues often reflect your emotional state. Once identified, label your feeling accurately. Use specific terms rather than vague descriptors. Instead of saying you feel 'bad', label it as 'frustrated', 'overwhelmed', or 'anxious'. This deliberate act of labelling increases emotional awareness.

Another useful technique is creating an emotion wheel—a visual representation of emotions categorised into primary and secondary feelings. By using this wheel, you can identify more granular emotions and understand how they relate to your experiences. Something as simple as feeling 'mildly annoyed' can be placed within the broader category of 'anger'. When exploring your emotional experiences, this visual aid serves as a valuable reference point, making identification more manageable and straightforward.

As you become more adept at recognising and labelling your emotions, consider developing an emotional vocabulary. Include a range of both simple and complex emotions, such as disappointment, ecstasy, curiosity, conflict, and disheartenment.

The Power of Becoming

The more specific your vocabulary, the clearer your understanding of your emotional world becomes. This clarity empowers you to communicate your feelings more effectively with others.

Practising mindfulness also enhances emotional recognition. Mindfulness involves directing attention to the present moment in an open, non-judgemental way. This practice allows you to observe thoughts and emotions without becoming overwhelmed. Regular mindfulness exercises, such as deep breathing or meditation, help ground you and improve emotional awareness. When we allow ourselves to remain present with our feelings, even uncomfortable ones, we can better navigate their complexities.

Once we learn to recognise and label our emotions, the next step is cultivating a response. This is where emotional mastery truly blossoms. Our immediate reactions often stem from automatic patterns developed over time—patterns that may not always serve us well. By recognising these tendencies, we can choose healthier responses. For instance, if frustration arises at work, rather than reacting with irritation, take a moment to breathe and reconsider your approach. This conscious practice enables more thoughtful responses that align with your goals and values.

Developing practices for emotional regulation, such as breathing exercises or grounding techniques, is also beneficial. When emotions drive decisions unchecked, impulsive choices often follow. Simple techniques that encourage calm can bridge the gap between emotion and conscious action. Deep, intentional breathing fosters a physiological state of relaxation that counters anxiety, allowing more rational processing. Grounding techniques, which reconnect us with our bodies and surroundings, can be particularly useful during emotionally charged moments.

Finally, foster a habit of reflection after emotionally intense experiences. Take time to contemplate how you felt, what triggered those feelings, and how you responded. Reflection illuminates patterns, offering insight into how various situations impact you. Discussing these reflections with a trusted confidant, therapist, or coach can provide valuable insights and perspectives. Honest dialogue about emotions cultivates both emotional intelligence and vulnerability, strengthening human connection.

In summary, understanding emotions is a fundamental step towards achieving emotional mastery. By recognising and labelling our feelings, we develop the awareness necessary for personal growth. Emotional intelligence encompasses self-awareness, self-regulation, motivation, empathy, and social skills—each contributing to our ability to navigate the emotional landscape effectively. Employing specific techniques such as emotional check-ins, emotion wheels, mindfulness, and reflection cultivates a deeper understanding of ourselves and enriches our interactions with others.

Emotional mastery is not merely about managing emotions; it is about transforming our relationship with them. The journey towards mastery requires patience and often involves confronting discomfort. However, as we strive to understand and embrace our emotions, we lay the groundwork for a life marked by growth, resilience, and connection. Through emotional mastery, we can become the best versions of ourselves—equipped to face challenges with grace and authenticity. By harnessing the power of our emotions, we unlock our fullest potential. It is within this transformative space that the power of becoming truly flourishes.

Transforming Anxiety into Fuel

The Power of Becoming

Anxiety is a universal experience, one that many of us face in various forms throughout our lives. It is a sensation that can range from mild unease to crushing panic, often leading to reluctance or an overwhelming desire to escape. Traditionally, anxiety has garnered a negative reputation, seen as something to be avoided or eliminated. However, what if we could reframe this narrative? What if anxiety could be transformed into a source of power—a catalyst for personal growth and transformation?

This subchapter delves into the art of transforming anxiety into fuel. The goal is to equip you with the tools to shift your relationship with anxiety, viewing it not as a hindrance but as an ally on your journey towards becoming your best self. By the end of this exploration, you will have a better understanding of how to channel anxiety productively and learn from the stories of those who have successfully made this shift, drawing inspiration from their journeys.

Anxiety often stems from uncertainty—the fear of the unknown. It can loom large in our minds when we face new challenges or significant life changes. However, instead of allowing anxiety to paralyse us, we can choose to redirect its energy. This transformative perspective can create pathways to resilience, motivating us to confront fears we might otherwise avoid.

The first step in transforming anxiety into fuel is recognising and acknowledging its presence. Rather than suppressing feelings of anxiety, we must learn to sit with them, observe them, and understand their signals. Why is this emotion arising? What underlying fears are surfacing? Practising mindfulness can aid profoundly in this discovery. Allowing yourself to sit in silence for a few moments each day helps you tune into your inner dialogue.

Ask yourself what you are feeling and why. From there, you can begin to navigate your anxiety more effectively.

Once you have acknowledged your anxious feelings, the next step is to reframe how you perceive anxiety itself. Instead of viewing it as an intruder, consider it a messenger. Anxiety signifies that something is important to you, often highlighting your values and desires. For instance, feeling anxious about a job interview likely indicates that you care about your career and want to make a positive impression. Repeating affirmations that embrace this perspective can be powerful. Remind yourself: 'This anxiety shows I care about my performance.'

From here, explore practical exercises designed to channel anxiety into actionable plans and concrete motivation. One effective method involves setting specific, achievable goals that align with the sources of your anxiety. If you find yourself anxious about public speaking, create a step-by-step action plan that breaks down the process into manageable steps. Start by visualising success, then write down your speech and practise in front of a mirror. Gradually raise the stakes—practise in front of friends or family and seek constructive feedback. This incremental approach allows you to view anxiety as a guide to growth rather than a barrier to it.

Another powerful exercise involves harnessing physical movement to manage anxiety. Engaging in regular physical activity—whether yoga, jogging, or dance—helps release pent-up energy and builds resilience against anxious feelings. Create a routine that incorporates movement you enjoy, making it a vital part of your strategy to harness the energy of anxiety. When you feel adrenaline surging, redirect it into a productive outlet such as going for a run, participating in a fitness class, or practising a martial art.

This shift not only alleviates anxiety in the moment but also empowers your mind and body to work together holistically, fortifying your resilience.

Mindfulness meditation can also play a significant role in transforming anxiety. By dedicating time to breathe deeply and focus your thoughts, you can ground yourself in the present moment, allowing anxious sensations to pass without judgment. Try incorporating a daily mindfulness practice into your routine, whether through guided meditation apps, local classes, or online resources. As you cultivate this discipline, you will find it easier to notice anxiety as an experience rather than an all-consuming reality.

Additionally, journalling can be an invaluable tool in transforming your relationship with anxiety. Write about your experiences—what triggers it, how it makes you feel, and how it impacts your decisions. Reflecting on these entries can uncover patterns, enabling you to reclaim your narrative around anxiety. Consider incorporating gratitude journalling; by acknowledging what you are thankful for, you can shift focus from anxiety to appreciation, fostering a more positive outlook.

Case studies provide powerful evidence of transformation through anxiety. Consider the story of Sarah, a woman in her thirties who, after losing her job, was engulfed by anxiety about her future. Instead of succumbing to despair, she used her anxiety as a beacon guiding her towards a long-held dream of becoming a writer. Channelling her anxiety into structured writing sessions, she began blogging about her career journey. Within months, Sarah not only secured a new job but also discovered a passion for storytelling, leading to freelance writing opportunities. Her anxiety had ignited a creative fire, propelling her towards a fulfilling path she had previously avoided.

In another case, we find Jason, whose anxiety around social interactions hindered his professional growth. Instead of withdrawing from networking opportunities, he embraced his anxious feelings while attending industry events. He coached himself to view these situations as chances to connect rather than prove himself worthy. By engaging in conversations with this new mindset, Jason transformed moments of anxiety into meaningful interactions that eventually led to new partnerships and career opportunities.

These stories highlight that anxiety is not solely a struggle but a multifaceted experience that can be cultivated for growth. By adopting this perspective and applying the practical exercises mentioned, anyone can begin transforming anxiety into motivational fuel. The next time anxiety arises, remember that it need not be a roadblock; it can serve as a stepping stone towards your goals, values, and personal evolution.

Finally, consider implementing a support system to facilitate transformation. Engage with mentors, therapists, or supportive friends who understand your journey and can reinforce your commitment to this new perspective. Sharing your experiences and setbacks can forge community connections and yield valuable insights, enriching your emotional mastery.

In conclusion, transforming anxiety into fuel requires intention, shifting perspectives, and implementing actionable strategies. By acknowledging and reframing your relationship with anxiety, you can harness it as a catalyst for growth. Practise mindfulness, set achievable goals, engage in physical activities, and document your journey through journalling. Recognise that anxiety can serve as a powerful tool guiding you towards your best self. As you become more adept at managing this emotion, you will find that each experience with anxiety can propel you further along your journey of becoming.

Joy as a Practice

In the landscape of emotional mastery, the concept of joy often feels like an elusive treasure—sought after yet difficult to grasp. Many people associate joy with transient moments—such as celebrations, achievements, or fleeting pleasures—believing it arises spontaneously rather than through intentional action. However, cultivating joy is indeed a practice, one that requires dedication, mindfulness, and a willingness to engage with the world in a positive manner.

In this subchapter, we explore the conscious cultivation of joy through practices such as gratitude journalling and mindfulness, highlighting how these methods enhance emotional well-being and create a more joyful existence.

Joy is more than a fleeting reaction to pleasurable experiences; it is a state of being that can be fostered through intentional effort. Scientific studies have shown that engaging in practices that promote joy can lead to significant improvements in overall well-being. Our brains are wired to seek pleasure—a primal mechanism for survival—but many of us become disconnected from the deeper joy that comes from within. To truly harness the power of joy, we must learn to navigate our emotions, acknowledging that true happiness is achievable through deliberate choices.

The Power of Becoming

One of the most powerful tools for cultivating joy is gratitude journalling. This practice involves regularly documenting the things we are thankful for, allowing us to shift focus from what we lack to what we cherish. Gratitude opens a gateway to joy, enabling us to appreciate the richness of life even in the midst of challenges. Research consistently shows that individuals who engage in gratitude practices report higher levels of positivity and resilience. They experience reduced feelings of anxiety and depression and enhanced overall life satisfaction.

Creating a gratitude journal is a simple yet profound act of self-care. It can be as minimal or as elaborate as you wish. To begin, find a quiet space—perhaps with a warm cup of tea or coffee—and take a moment to reflect on your day or your life in general. What small joys did you experience? Perhaps it was a heartfelt conversation with a friend, the beauty of nature during your walk, or the warmth of a smile from a stranger. The beauty of this practice lies in its simplicity; it does not require grand achievements, but rather encourages you to notice and appreciate the ordinary moments that often go overlooked.

As you write, describe not only the events you are grateful for but also the feelings associated with them. This emotional connection deepens the experience and imprints joy more firmly into your mind. Recording gratitude serves as a reminder of the positivity that exists in your life, providing a vital counterbalance to the negativity that surrounds us. Over time, this practice helps retrain your brain to recognise joy in everyday life, transforming your emotional landscape.

In addition to gratitude journalling, mindfulness stands as another powerful approach to cultivating joy. Mindfulness is the practice of being fully present in the moment, observing thoughts and feelings without judgment or attachment. When we cultivate mindfulness, we connect with our experiences authentically, allowing joy to emerge naturally from within.

Mindfulness can take many forms: meditation, breathing exercises, or simply pausing to absorb the sights, sounds, and sensations of your surroundings. It encourages curiosity about the present moment, shifting focus away from worries of the past or anxieties about the future. By immersing ourselves fully in our experiences, we permit ourselves to savour even the smallest pleasures.

Consider a moment when you are enjoying a meal. Instead of eating mindlessly, take the time to engage with your food. Observe the colours, textures, and aromas. As you take your first bite, allow yourself to experience the flavours and the satisfaction of nourishing your body. This practice can transform a mundane routine into a moment of celebration. When we practise mindfulness, we learn to appreciate the beauty in life's simplest pleasures, enabling us to tap into a deeper sense of joy.

The interplay between gratitude and mindfulness creates a robust framework for joy. When we practise gratitude, we often find ourselves more present and aware of our surroundings, allowing joy to flourish. Simultaneously, mindfulness enhances our ability to recognise moments of joy, making it easier to express gratitude for them. Together, these practices form potent tools in our emotional mastery toolkit, helping us cultivate a more joyful existence.

Engaging narratives illustrate the power of joy. Consider Sarah, who had spent years overwhelmed by life's pressures. Balancing a demanding job, raising her children, and managing her household left her depleted and disconnected. A friend introduced her to gratitude journalling. Sceptical yet intrigued, she began jotting down three things she appreciated each day.

At first, it felt like a chore, but as the weeks passed, she began to notice subtle shifts in her perspective. She began to savour her morning coffee; her children's laughter resonated on a deeper level. Gradually, journalling became a delightful ritual. Within months, Sarah felt a profound change within herself. Her days were filled with joy she had once overlooked, and she developed a newfound resilience in the face of life's challenges.

Similarly, Mark, who had struggled with anxiety for much of his adult life, discovered mindfulness meditation through a friend. Initially resistant, he committed to sitting quietly for ten minutes each morning. To his surprise, he found a space where his thoughts could settle. Over time, mindfulness not only calmed his mind but opened a door to joy he had never known. Simple moments—a bird's song, sunlight on his skin—became sources of inspiration. The world around him transformed into a canvas of joy, enriching his well-being.

Both Sarah's and Mark's journeys illustrate that consciously engaging in practices that cultivate joy can lead to profound transformation. Joy is not a distant dream but a reachable state of being. By pursuing gratitude and mindfulness with dedication, we learn to embrace joy as a steadfast companion, one we can return to again and again.

As we deepen our emotional mastery, it becomes clear that cultivating joy is an ongoing process, one we must incorporate into our daily lives with intention and commitment. The beauty of these practices lies in their accessibility; anyone can engage in gratitude journalling or mindfulness at any stage of life. The key is to prioritise them, allowing joy to become a cornerstone of emotional well-being.

To make joy a continual practice, consider creating a joy plan—a personal blueprint that includes gratitude and mindfulness activities tailored to your preferences. Designate specific times each day for these practices, such as journaling in the morning, taking mindful walks at lunch, or dedicating an evening to reflection. By weaving joy into the fabric of your daily routine, you reinforce its importance and make it an integral part of your life.

Remember, joy is inherently infectious. As you cultivate joy within yourself, you will likely inspire others to do the same. Your positive outlook may encourage friends, family, and colleagues to adopt a happier perspective, creating a ripple effect that enhances the emotional well-being of your community. The more we practise joy, the more it spreads, transforming individual lives and collective spirit.

Recognising obstacles that may hinder the practice of joy is equally crucial. Life presents challenges that can make it difficult to feel grateful or present. Difficult moments, losses, or major changes can cast shadows over our emotions, making joy seem distant and elusive. During such times, acknowledge your feelings and extend compassion to yourself. Remember that joy and sadness can coexist; embracing the full spectrum of emotion is essential to mastery.

It can also be helpful to revisit the roots of your joy—the things that first sparked happiness in your life. Consider how certain experiences or relationships contributed to your joy in the past. This reflection becomes valuable during challenging periods, reminding you that joy is always within reach, even if it feels far away.

In conclusion, joy as a practice invites us to engage regularly and intentionally with our emotional well-being. Through gratitude journalling and mindfulness, we can cultivate a deeper connection to joy, transforming it from a fleeting emotion into a foundational part of our lives. The stories of individuals like Sarah and Mark remind us that the path to joy is both navigable and rewarding, proving that happiness is not merely a fleeting feeling but a conscious choice.

Embracing joy requires effort, but the rewards are immeasurable. By committing to this practice, we open ourselves to limitless possibilities, creating a joyful existence that enriches our lives and touches those around us. Let us embark on this journey and choose joy not only as an emotion but as a deliberate practice—a commitment to emotional mastery and a testament to the beauty of becoming our best selves.

The Discipline of Focus

Identifying Your Priorities

The journey towards becoming your best self is filled with opportunities and challenges—a complex tapestry woven through the choices you make each day. Among the most crucial skills you will cultivate in this process is the ability to prioritise effectively.

In a world swamped with distractions, obligations, and ever-increasing demands on your time, identifying what truly matters becomes an essential practice for ensuring that your focus aligns with your goals and values. This subchapter explores how to navigate the labyrinth of choices and commitments, emphasising the importance of prioritisation in your quest for personal growth.

At its core, prioritisation is about making conscious choices based on your values, aspirations, and intended outcomes. Without a clear sense of what is genuinely important, it is easy to become trapped in the whirlwind of daily tasks, losing sight of the broader vision you hold for your life. You may find yourself caught between urgent deadlines and meaningful activities, leading to frustration, stress, and an overwhelming sense of being scattered.

One powerful tool for gaining clarity is the Eisenhower Matrix, developed by former U.S. President Dwight D. Eisenhower. This framework helps you categorise tasks based on their urgency and importance, guiding you on when to act, delegate, or let go of tasks altogether.

The matrix divides tasks into four quadrants:

1. Urgent and Important: Tasks that require immediate attention and align with your core goals. These should be your top priority.

2. Important but Not Urgent: Tasks that contribute to your long-term objectives but can be scheduled for later. Prioritising these helps you make steady progress towards your aspirations.

3. Urgent but Not Important: Tasks that are pressing but do not contribute significantly to your overarching goals. Delegate or limit time spent on these.

4. Neither Urgent nor Important: Activities that provide little or no value to your growth. Recognising these can be liberating, freeing time and energy for what truly matters.

As you engage with this framework, consider how it applies to your current life situation. Begin by listing your tasks for the upcoming week. Once identified, categorise each using the matrix, assessing both urgency and importance. This process clarifies your immediate priorities and highlights areas where you may be spending time on tasks that do not align with your goals or values.

Reflective exercises play a crucial role in guiding this self-assessment. Take a moment to reflect on your current focus areas. Ask yourself: What activities fill my days? How do they align with my values and long-term vision? What constitutes success for me? These questions provide insight into whether your actions reflect your authentic self or if they are merely reactions to external pressures.

The Power of Becoming

As you work through your list, be mindful of how each task connects to your core values. Reflect on whether you are honouring those values through your daily actions or compromising them to meet expectations. If you discover discrepancies between your tasks and your principles, it may be time to re-evaluate your commitments. Honest reflection often reveals underlying beliefs that drive your choices.

Here are some guiding questions for reflection:

1. What do I value most in my life? Whether it is family, health, career, or personal growth, identifying your core values is a foundational step in prioritisation.

2. What are my long-term goals? Clarifying your aspirations helps determine which activities contribute to growth and fulfilment.

3. Am I reacting to what others expect of me? Consider whether certain tasks are rooted in societal or external pressures rather than your own ambitions. Learning to say no to these can be a form of empowerment.

4. Which tasks energise me, and which drain me? Recognising this distinction enables you to allocate time more effectively, focusing on what invigorates and inspires you.

Once you have completed your reflection, visualise where your focus currently lies. Are you drawn to urgent tasks, leaving little time for those that are important but not pressing? If so, you may find yourself in a reactionary loop—perpetually addressing what demands immediate attention while neglecting what could significantly enhance your life's trajectory.

To shift focus from urgency to importance, consider setting weekly or monthly goals. Establish SMART objectives—specific, measurable, achievable, relevant, and time-bound—that align with your long-term vision. Break these larger goals into actionable steps that can be integrated into your daily routine. This process not only helps define what is important but also reinforces consistency in prioritising those tasks.

As you embark on this prioritisation journey, remember that it is not merely about productivity or checking boxes on a to-do list. It is about making deliberate choices that resonate with your values and aspirations. Being intentional with your time allows you to devote energy to activities that foster growth and bring you closer to the person you strive to become.

Another key aspect of prioritising is learning to be flexible. Life is unpredictable, and sometimes the unexpected will require you to shift focus. When these moments arise, a clear understanding of your core priorities enables you to adapt without losing sight of your goals. Flexibility fosters resilience, enabling you to adapt while staying aligned with your overall vision.

It is also vital to communicate your priorities clearly with others. Sharing your goals and the reasons behind your choices can strengthen relationships and garner support from those around you. When others understand your commitment to personal growth, they are more likely to respect your time and decisions.

In addition to the Eisenhower Matrix, consider other frameworks that resonate with you. The Pareto Principle, or the 80/20 rule, suggests that 80% of your results come from 20% of your efforts. Identifying the few activities that yield the most significant impact helps you channel focus more effectively, ensuring that your energy is spent on what truly matters.

As we explore the art of prioritisation, it becomes essential to establish boundaries around your time and energy. Prioritisation often requires learning to say no. Although difficult, refusing commitments that do not align with your values or distract from your goals is an empowering act. Boundaries not only protect your time but also send a clear message to others about your dedication to personal growth.

To sharpen your skill in saying no, practise assertiveness. Remember, you cannot please everyone, and it is vital to honour your authentic self. Developing the ability to communicate your needs firmly and respectfully fosters healthier relationships while allowing you to reclaim time for your priorities.

In addition to boundaries, surrounding yourself with a supportive environment can bolster your focus. Be mindful of the influences in your life. Are the people around you uplifting, encouraging, and aligned with your values? Or do they drain your energy and distract you from your intentions? Evaluating your social circle is crucial in reinforcing your commitment to becoming the best version of yourself.

As you refine your priorities, be patient with yourself. This is not a race but a journey. Self-growth is a gradual process, and regularly reassessing your priorities helps you adjust as needed. Celebrate small victories along the way, acknowledging your progress and the lessons you learn. As you grow more attuned to your priorities, you will find it easier to maintain focus and align your actions with your aspirations.

Embrace the notion that prioritisation is an ongoing practice, not a one-time task. Life will continue to present new challenges and opportunities, each demanding your attention and evaluation. By honing your prioritisation skills, you equip yourself with the tools needed to navigate life's complexities, ensuring that you are always moving towards your best self.

Finally, as you look ahead, remind yourself of the ultimate purpose behind your priorities: becoming who you are meant to be. Prioritisation is not merely about time management; it is about cultivating a life that aligns with your inner truth. Each choice refines your character and steers you closer to fulfilling your unique purpose.

In conclusion, identifying your priorities is a crucial exercise in cultivating focus. By utilising frameworks like the Eisenhower Matrix, engaging in reflective practices, setting actionable goals, and establishing healthy boundaries, you can gain clarity on what truly matters. This clarity liberates you from the noise of distraction, allowing you to navigate the path of personal growth with intention and ease.

Remember, the journey of becoming is a lifelong endeavour filled with learning and discovery. Embrace it fully, and let your priorities guide you towards a life of purpose and fulfilment.

Embracing Mindfulness

In our fast-paced, hyper-connected world, distractions are an ever-present challenge that pulls our attention in countless directions. The rise of technology has undoubtedly enriched our lives, but it has also sown the seeds of impatience, anxiety, and scattered focus. As we navigate our daily routines, it is easy to become caught up in the rush, glossing over experiences that warrant our full attention. This is where the practice of mindfulness enters the scene, offering a powerful antidote to the chaos.

Mindfulness is the art of being present, fully aware and engaged with the current moment without judgment. It invites us to pause, to notice what we perceive, and to connect more deeply with ourselves and the world around us. When we embrace mindfulness, we cultivate an acute awareness of our thoughts, emotions, and sensations, allowing us to become more attuned to our distractions and, subsequently, more skilled in managing them.

This subchapter will explore various mindfulness techniques, underscoring their role in enhancing focus, reducing distractions, and integrating mindfulness into our lives.

To understand the transformative potential of mindfulness, consider a narrative that encapsulates its essence. Imagine a busy office environment where deadlines loom large, emails flood in, and the demands of colleagues pull you in multiple directions. In the midst of this whirlwind, one employee, Sarah, decides to experiment with mindfulness.

Taking a deep breath, Sarah closes her eyes for a moment. She brings her attention back to her breath, feeling the cool air enter her nostrils and the warmth as she exhales. As she engages in this simple practice, Sarah becomes aware of the tightness in her shoulders and the swirling thoughts telling her she should be doing more. Yet instead of allowing herself to be swept away by the chaos, she acknowledges these feelings and gently redirects her focus back to her breath.

The Power of Becoming

Through this brief encounter with mindfulness, Sarah discovers that she can step back from the frantic pace of her work. She learns to observe her thoughts without becoming tangled in them, recognising that they are not necessarily true but reflections of her current state. By cultivating this practice, Sarah begins to chip away at her distractions, gradually enhancing her ability to concentrate for longer periods. She finds that this newfound focus not only improves her productivity but also enhances her overall well-being.

So, how can we integrate mindfulness into our daily routines, much like Sarah did? Below are several practical techniques designed to enhance focus and reduce distractions in our busy lives.

One of the most popular mindfulness practices is meditation. Meditation, though often misunderstood as complex or inaccessible, can be as simple as spending a few minutes each day in stillness. To begin a meditation practice, find a quiet space where you can sit comfortably. Set a timer for five to ten minutes and close your eyes. Focus your attention on your breath: observe its rhythm and the sensation of the air entering and leaving your body. When your mind wanders, as it inevitably will, gently guide your focus back to your breath. This exercise cultivates concentration and calm. As you become familiar with the practice, you may find it easier to maintain attention during more challenging tasks.

Another powerful technique is the body scan. This exercise enhances our connection to the body, fostering awareness of physical sensations and enabling us to release tension. To perform a body scan, lie down comfortably and take a few deep breaths. Then bring your awareness to each part of your body, starting from your toes and moving upward to the crown of your head. Notice any areas of tension, discomfort, or relaxation. What thoughts arise as you move through your body? By bringing mindfulness to your physical self, you create space for relaxation and can approach tasks with a clearer, more focused mind.

Mindful walking is another practice that supports mindfulness in daily life. This can be particularly effective for those who find meditation challenging or who prefer movement as a way to centre themselves. During a mindful walk, focus on the sensation of your feet hitting the ground, the rhythm of your steps, and the sensory details around you: the sound of birds, the breeze on your skin, or the colours of the leaves. As you engage with your surroundings, you redirect your attention away from mental clutter. Even a simple stroll can become a meditative experience, grounding you in the present moment and enhancing focus.

Mindfulness can also be woven into everyday tasks such as eating or washing dishes. For example, during a meal, savour each bite. Notice the flavours, textures, and aromas of your food. Eat slowly, setting aside distractions such as your phone or television. This not only promotes mindful eating but can aid digestion and enhance enjoyment. When washing dishes, immerse yourself in the sensory experience: the feel of warm, soapy water, the sound of utensils clinking, and the satisfaction of cleaning a plate. By bringing mindfulness into routine activities, you reinforce the habit of being present and gradually train your mind to focus more effectively.

Another key aspect of mindfulness is the nurturing of self-compassion. As we practise being aware of our thoughts and feelings without judgment, we develop a kinder relationship with ourselves. When distractions arise, such as a wave of self-doubt or negative self-talk, we can acknowledge them with gentleness.

Mindfulness helps us recognise that everyone struggles with distraction and that it is a natural part of the human experience. This shift in perspective alleviates pressure, enabling us to return to tasks with renewed clarity.

In a world where our attention is perpetually divided, mindfulness is a potent tool for reclaiming focus. Research has shown that regular mindfulness practice can enhance attention span, improve cognitive flexibility, and broaden creative capacity. Individuals who practise mindfulness demonstrate greater control over their attention, leading to improved performance on tasks requiring sustained focus.

As we cultivate mindfulness, we should not be discouraged by setbacks. Mindfulness is not about perfection; it is about embracing a journey toward awareness. Like Sarah, who initially struggled with distractions, we too will experience ebb and flow as we integrate mindfulness into our lives. There will be days when distractions feel overwhelming, but each moment of practice prepares us to respond with resilience.

To reinforce mindfulness, consider creating a schedule. Dedicate specific times each day for intentional mindfulness exercises, whether five minutes of meditation in the morning or a mindful walk at lunch. Establishing a routine affirms your commitment, gradually embedding mindfulness into daily life. You may also wish to journal your experiences, reflecting on how mindfulness impacts your focus and attention over time. This can help track progress and provide motivation.

Incorporating mindfulness into group settings can amplify its impact. Whether in a workplace, school, or community organisation,

The Power of Becoming

collective mindfulness practices such as group meditation or mindful discussions can foster a culture of focus, collaboration, and well-being. When individuals share experiences of mindfulness, they enhance not only their own growth but that of the group, creating a ripple effect of positive change.

Mindfulness also intersects with the importance of taking breaks. Research in cognitive psychology supports the idea that short breaks, when approached mindfully, can enhance productivity. After a period of focused work, typically between 25 and 50 minutes, stepping away for a mindful break can rejuvenate the mind. Stretch, breathe deeply, or take a mindful walk. Such breaks help prevent burnout and keep focus sharp throughout the day.

In conclusion, embracing mindfulness is a powerful step toward enhancing focus and reducing distractions in our busy lives. Through techniques such as meditation, body scans, mindful walking, and integrating mindfulness into daily activities, we can cultivate a deep connection to the present moment. As we practise awareness and acceptance of our thoughts and emotions, we nurture self-compassion and improve overall well-being. Each moment dedicated to mindfulness strengthens focus and resilience, and while the journey may involve challenges, the rewards are profound.

The discipline of focus requires continual practice, and mindfulness is a steadfast ally. By integrating these techniques into daily routines, we learn to navigate distractions with grace, enabling us to grow and thrive. Embrace mindfulness not merely as an exercise but as a way of living: a lens through which to encounter each moment with intention, clarity, and presence. The journey of mindfulness is never truly finished; it unfolds continuously as we cherish the art of becoming.

Establishing Boundaries

Setting healthy boundaries is critical for maintaining focus. In a world filled with distractions, demands, and constant noise, the ability to establish and uphold boundaries allows us to regain control over our time and energy. This subchapter explores the essential role boundaries play in personal discipline, practical strategies for setting them effectively, and the empowerment that comes from learning to say no. As we navigate the various aspects of our lives, establishing clear boundaries enables us to prioritise what truly matters and safeguard our focus, thereby enhancing our journey toward becoming our best selves.

At the core of establishing boundaries is the recognition that our time, energy, and attention are finite resources. In both personal and professional life, we often find ourselves spread too thin, trying to meet the expectations of others while neglecting our own needs and goals. This imbalance compromises our ability to focus on tasks that are genuinely meaningful. Without boundaries, we risk becoming overwhelmed, stressed, and unfulfilled, ultimately hindering growth and transformation.

The concept of boundaries can be broken down into several key components, each playing a vital role in enhancing focus and personal discipline. These components include physical boundaries, emotional boundaries, and time boundaries. Understanding and implementing these effectively is crucial for creating an environment where focus can thrive.

Physical boundaries relate to the space we occupy and how we manage our environment. This includes our workspaces, homes, and even the broader settings we move within. One practical approach is to create a designated area for focused work that is free from distractions. This might mean setting up a home office or choosing a specific spot in a café that signals to you and others that you are in a focused state. By removing clutter, minimising distractions, and ensuring that your environment is conducive to concentration, you cultivate a physical space that supports your goal of maintaining focus.

Emotional boundaries, on the other hand, pertain to how we engage with others and protect our emotional well-being. It is essential to recognise when our emotional energy is being drained, often by individuals who may not respect our time or limitations. Learning to communicate emotional boundaries can be challenging, especially for those who are naturally accommodating. However, articulating these boundaries is key to preserving focus. This might involve having difficult conversations with friends, family, or coworkers about your need for privacy, support, or space. Establishing emotional boundaries helps guard mental energy and prioritise emotional health, which directly impacts our capacity to concentrate on our goals.

Time boundaries are another crucial aspect. They dictate how we allocate our time to various activities. Without them, we may find ourselves overcommitting to obligations that detract from our ability to focus. Setting clear working hours, prioritising tasks, and scheduling breaks are effective strategies. Using tools such as time-blocking can help you create a structured plan that delineates when you will focus on specific tasks and when you will step away to recharge. This not only increases productivity but also empowers you to manage your time more effectively.

To further empower ourselves in setting boundaries, it is important to enhance our ability to say no. For many, saying no can feel uncomfortable, potentially leading to guilt or fear of disappointing others. However, saying no is critical in safeguarding our focus. When we decline requests that do not align with our priorities or goals, we make room for opportunities that resonate with our values.

Communicating boundaries with assertiveness and clarity is fundamental. Consider simple, direct responses that honour both your needs and the needs of others. For example, if a colleague asks for assistance on a project when you are already committed, you might respond, "I appreciate you thinking of me, but I need to focus on my current priorities right now." Such responses validate the request while firmly asserting your boundary.

Practising saying no in low-stakes situations can help build confidence. Start small. If a friend invites you to an event that you do not wish to attend, practise declining politely with gratitude. The more you practise, the more comfortable you will become in upholding boundaries in higher-stakes situations.

It is also important to understand that communication about boundaries is a two-way street. To cultivate healthy relationships, we must invite open dialogue about boundaries with those around us. This fosters mutual respect and creates an environment where everyone feels comfortable expressing their needs. Conversations about boundaries, expectations, and limitations can strengthen relationships and enhance focus.

As we navigate life's complexities, we must remain vigilant about the boundaries we set. This vigilance involves reflecting regularly on whether our boundaries are being respected and whether they need adjustment. Life is dynamic, and what served as a healthy boundary at one time may need revision in another context.

Periodically assessing boundaries empowers us to remain proactive in safeguarding focus.

Another aspect to consider is the impact of technology. In the digital age, drawing clear lines between work and personal life has become increasingly challenging. The expectation to remain constantly connected often leads to blurred boundaries, making it difficult to focus on the present moment. To counter this, it is essential to establish digital boundaries, such as setting specific times to check emails or social media, or turning off notifications during focused work periods. By controlling your interaction with technology, you minimise distractions and strengthen concentration.

Mindfulness also plays a crucial role in establishing and maintaining boundaries. By cultivating mindfulness, you develop greater awareness of your needs and limitations, ensuring that your boundaries reflect your true priorities. Techniques like meditation, deep-breathing exercises, or brief moments of reflection throughout the day help you check in with yourself. This self-awareness aids you in recognising when boundaries are being approached or violated.

As you deepen your understanding of boundaries, it is important to acknowledge the emotional responses that may arise when asserting them. Feelings of guilt, anxiety, or fear of conflict are common when first learning to set boundaries. Recognise these emotions as part of the process. The key is to practise self-compassion and remind yourself that establishing boundaries is an act of self-care. It is reasonable to prioritise your focus and well-being, and doing so ultimately leads to healthier relationships and greater fulfilment.

Another practical approach to reinforcing boundaries is involving a support system. Surrounding yourself with individuals who respect your boundaries and encourage your progress can strengthen your commitment. Share your goals and the boundaries you wish to establish with supportive friends or family members who can help keep you accountable. A strong support network offers encouragement during challenges and accountability in honouring your boundaries.

Be prepared for pushback. Not everyone will accept your boundaries immediately, especially if they are used to a different dynamic. In such cases, it is essential to stand firm but gracious in your communication, reiterating why your boundaries are necessary for your well-being. Consistency is vital. Over time, when you uphold your limits, people begin to respect and understand them.

In addition to empowering yourself, consider how you can be mindful of others' boundaries. Practising empathy and respect toward the boundaries of those you interact with fosters a culture of understanding and support. This dynamic not only strengthens your connections but also encourages others to reflect on their own boundaries and focus.

Setting healthy boundaries is one of the most effective strategies for ensuring a disciplined approach to focus, as it allows us to prioritise what truly matters. By establishing physical, emotional, and time boundaries; enhancing our ability to say no; and utilising mindfulness and support systems, we create a solid foundation for personal growth and transformation. The journey toward becoming your best self is inherently tied to the ability to protect your focus, and setting boundaries is a powerful tool in that pursuit.

Take a moment to assess your current boundaries and consider the changes you can make to safeguard your focus. Every step you take in this direction brings you closer to realising your potential and living a life aligned with your true ambitions and values.

The Strength of Character

Defining Integrity and Its Role in Growth

Integrity is a term that often gets tossed around in discussions about character, ethics, and personal growth. But what does integrity truly mean? At its core, integrity is the quality of being honest and having strong moral principles. It is the alignment of one's actions with one's values and beliefs, creating a sense of authenticity that resonates deeply with oneself and with others. In a world rife with moral ambiguity and ethical dilemmas, the necessity of integrity cannot be overstated; it becomes the backbone of one's character and serves as a foundation upon which personal growth can be built.

When we examine integrity, we see that it manifests in various aspects of life. It signifies adherence to moral and ethical principles and a commitment to doing what one believes is right, even when it is challenging. Imagine a lawyer who refuses to take on a case she knows is unjust, or a business leader who chooses transparency over profit maximisation, even at the cost of short-term gains. These choices are reflections of integrity, acts that align closely with one's values and the willingness to stand by those values regardless of external pressures.

The role of integrity in personal growth is profound. It shapes not only how individuals view themselves but also how they are perceived by others. When integrity is present, trust is established. Trust is a currency in our interpersonal relationships and professional collaborations. It allows for deeper connections and fosters an environment where open communication can flourish. For example, consider a team at work where members are encouraged to express their ideas honestly without fear of judgment or reprisal. The presence of integrity within the team creates a safe space that promotes innovation, creativity, and collective problem-solving. Each member feels valued and respected, leading to stronger collaboration and a sense of shared purpose.

Furthermore, integrity enhances relationships by fostering an atmosphere of respect and accountability. When people witness integrity in action, they are more likely to emulate that behaviour themselves. This ripple effect can create a culture of integrity within families, communities, organisations, and societies. Take a moment to reflect on a mentor or role model who exemplifies integrity. Their actions likely inspire and motivate you to lead a life guided by your values. As you aspire to grow, surrounding yourself with individuals of integrity can have a transformative impact, both on your journey and in your approach to relationships.

In essence, integrity is a guiding compass. It shapes decisions, influences behaviour, and directs one's path in life. Authenticity is a hallmark of integrity. When you act in ways that are congruent with your values, you send a powerful message both to yourself and to others. This alignment nurtures self-esteem and confidence, as individuals become more comfortable in their own skin. Knowing that your actions reflect your true self empowers you to navigate the complexities of life with conviction and clarity.

Consider the story of Maya, a young professional who found herself in a morally ambiguous situation at her workplace. Tasked with delivering a project that included misleading information, she faced a dilemma. Staying silent could benefit her career in the short run, but she knew that doing so would undermine her values. Maya chose to speak up, advocating for the truth and suggesting an alternative approach that aligned with her ethical beliefs. Though it was a difficult decision that initially put her at odds with some colleagues, demonstrating integrity resulted in her gaining respect and trust from her peers and superiors alike.

Authenticity in actions shapes one's destiny. When we make decisions based on integrity, we are not only crafting our own destiny but also influencing the world around us in a meaningful way. Every ethical choice propels us forward on our growth journey while also setting a standard for those who cross our paths. Think about moments in your life where you acted out of integrity; those instances likely stand out as pivotal experiences. They may have opened doors, strengthened relationships, or provided clarity in times of uncertainty.

As you contemplate the role of integrity in your own life, consider the following questions: What values are central to who you are? How do your actions reflect those values? Are there areas in your life where you compromise your integrity for the sake of convenience or approval? Engaging with these questions can foster a deeper understanding of how integrity aligns with your authentic self and ultimately shapes your growth.

Moreover, integrity is not a static quality; it is a dynamic process that evolves as we grow and learn. It requires ongoing reflection, self-awareness, and a willingness to confront uncomfortable truths about our behaviours and choices. Growth can be challenging, and sometimes our values may come into conflict with our desires. It is through this friction that the true strength of our character is tested, allowing us to recalibrate our actions and realign with our core beliefs.

The Power of Becoming

The cultivation of integrity necessitates commitment and practice. It involves placing value on honesty, being accountable for our choices, and acknowledging our mistakes without deflecting responsibility. Embracing integrity means staying true to oneself in moments of difficulty, ensuring that your actions never waver in the face of opposition. This steadfastness has the power to uplift you and inspire those around you, creating a chain reaction of positive influence.

An essential connection to consider is the relationship between integrity and personal growth. Integrity fosters an environment of openness, where mistakes can be acknowledged and learned from instead of concealed. This openness encourages individuals to take risks, embrace challenges, and pursue growth opportunities. In environments rooted in integrity, individuals are more likely to experiment, innovate, and develop resilience in the face of setbacks.

Imagine a community where integrity is upheld as a shared value. In such a space, individuals feel empowered to share ideas, take initiative, and collaborate without fear of judgment. They are not only accountable to themselves but also to one another. This shared commitment to integrity weaves a rich tapestry of trust, confidence, and mutual respect among community members, ultimately elevating the collective experience.

The importance of integrity extends beyond personal and relational domains; it also impacts professional and societal landscapes. In businesses, leaders who model integrity foster a culture where ethical behaviour prevails, resulting in increased employee satisfaction and loyalty, as well as enhanced brand reputation. Customers seek transparency and authenticity in the brands they support. Companies that embody integrity gain an invaluable competitive advantage in building trust with consumers.

In contrast, organisations lacking integrity often face dire consequences: loss of reputation, decreased morale, and disengagement from stakeholders. Scandals originating from ethical failures can erode customer loyalty and tarnish a brand's image. Reflecting on high-profile cases where integrity was compromised reveals a trend: the fallout affects not just the individuals involved but creates ripples that impact teams, companies, and even entire industries.

The world calls for leaders, innovators, and changemakers to navigate complexity through the lens of integrity. As individuals embrace integrity in their personal and professional lives, they not only chart their own course but also inspire others to do the same. The courage to align with one's values and speak out against wrongdoing can create monumental shifts and foster social progress.

Wrapping up this exploration of integrity, it is evident that true growth requires unwavering dedication to living a life of authenticity. As you continue your journey toward personal development, remember that the strength of your character lies in the integrity you actively practise. The small choices you make every day accumulate, forming a life of purpose and fulfilment. Strive to act in ways that reflect your principles; they will serve as your compass, guiding you through the intricacies of life and leading you toward your best self.

In nearly every aspect of life, integrity transforms interactions and nurtures growth. The question remains: will you answer the call? Will you rise to the occasion of embodying integrity, not just for your benefit but for the greater good? As you further define your values and commit to a path of authenticity, you will discover that strength in character grows through conscious choices and steadfast adherence to what is right. Ultimately, integrity does more than shape your identity; it carves out a legacy that will decisively influence those around you. Become the embodiment of integrity, and watch as the world around you begins to reflect the strength and depth of your character. Each step taken in authenticity brightens the path of not only your own journey but also those who follow, creating a tapestry of growth woven from shared values, trust, and resilient connections.

Building a Resilient Character

In the journey of becoming our best selves, character serves as the bedrock upon which we build our lives and navigate our experiences. Yet character alone is not enough; it must be tested, strengthened, and refined over time, particularly through adversity. Resilience, the ability to withstand, recover, and grow from difficult circumstances, plays a crucial role in this transformative process. Without resilience, values can become mere words on a page, easily forgotten or compromised when life presents its inevitable challenges.

In this exploration of resilient character, we will delve into the interplay between resilience and integrity, confront personal adversity, and discover the strength that upholding our values in tough times instills within us.

Resilience is not simply an innate trait; it is a skill that can be cultivated through intentional practice and reflection. At its core, resilience empowers individuals to confront obstacles without compromising their values. It fosters an unwavering commitment to what truly matters, even when faced with uncertainty or discomfort. This steadfastness can be observed in numerous individuals throughout history, people who stood firm in their convictions despite immense pressure to conform or give up. Their stories serve as powerful reminders of how resilience can fortify character and reinforce our sense of self.

Think of Nelson Mandela, who spent 27 years in prison for his stance against apartheid in South Africa. Rather than allow confinement to break his spirit or alter his principles, Mandela used that time to reflect, learn, and prepare for a future where he could lead his country toward equality. His resilience in the face of systemic injustice not only solidified his character but transformed him into a beacon of hope for millions. Mandela's unwavering dedication to his values, freedom, justice, and dignity, exemplifies how resilient individuals can maintain their integrity under even the most challenging circumstances.

In our everyday lives, we may not face the same scale of adversity as Mandela, but the challenges we encounter can threaten our commitment to our values just the same. A personal or professional setback, a betrayal by a trusted friend, or a moral dilemma at work can all test our character. This is where resilience becomes paramount. It allows us to make decisions aligned with our core values rather than succumbing to fear, anger, or despair.

Take, for example, the story of Dhruv, a young entrepreneur who launched a tech startup with the intention of making education accessible to underprivileged children. After years of hard work and sacrifice, Dhruv faced a severe setback when a major investor pulled out just before a crucial product launch. The pressure mounted, and many advised him to pivot away from his mission and focus solely on profitability. However, Dhruv chose to stay true to his values, believing that profit must not overshadow purpose. In the face of adversity, Dhruv's resilience shone through as he rallied his team, forged new partnerships, and sought alternative funding sources, all while keeping the mission of equitable education at the forefront of his efforts. His commitment not only salvaged the launch but also emphasised the importance of integrity in business. Through his struggles, Dhruv emerged not only with a successful venture but also with a deeper understanding of his character and purpose.

What can we learn from the stories of resilience surrounding us? Firstly, resilience requires self-awareness, a critical aspect of knowing ourselves. When we know our values, we are better equipped to defend them during turbulent times. We can reflect on what truly matters to us, why certain principles hold significance, and how we can uphold them in the face of challenges. Engaging in reflective practices, such as journaling, meditation, or thoughtful discussion with trusted friends, can enhance this self-awareness. By regularly evaluating our motivations and the alignment between our actions and our values, we build a resilient character that can navigate the ups and downs of life with confidence.

In addition, acknowledging and processing our emotions is crucial in developing resilience. Instead of suppressing feelings of fear, anger, or disappointment, we must face them head-on. Emotions are neither good nor bad; they are human. By embracing our emotional experiences and using them as fuel for growth, we can fortify our character. Consider the story of Maria, a dedicated nurse who witnessed the devastating effects of a pandemic on her patients and community. Amid the emotional toll, Maria faced immense pressure to either succumb to despair or find strength amidst the chaos. Rather than shying away from her emotions, Maria chose to lean into her compassion, using her empathetic nature as a source of resilience. She organised support groups for healthcare workers, advocating for mental health awareness and reminding others of the importance of emotional well-being during crises.

Maria's journey reveals that resilience is not a solitary endeavour; it flourishes through connection and community. Creating and maintaining relationships with those who share our values fortifies our character. When we surround ourselves with individuals who inspire us to uphold our ideals, we cultivate an environment of mutual support, encouraging resilience in ourselves and others. As we encounter difficulties, these connections serve as grounding reminders of our shared values and the strength that arises from unwavering commitment.

However, it is essential to acknowledge that the journey of resilience is not linear. There will be setbacks, and there may be times when we falter or question our values. In those moments, it is important to show ourselves grace and compassion. We are human, and every struggle is an opportunity for growth. Just as muscles strengthen through resistance, our character gains depth through the trials we encounter. Each setback can refine our understanding of ourselves, helping us recalibrate our values and reaffirm our commitment to them.

Practising resilience also involves adaptable thinking, an essential component of personal growth. Circumstances will inevitably change, but our values can remain a steadfast compass. By embracing a flexible approach, we can learn to navigate the shifts without losing sight of what truly matters to us. This adaptability

The Power of Becoming

can be cultivated through proactive problem-solving, creative thinking, and a willingness to evolve.

Reflecting on the journey of becoming resilient invites us to honour the struggle as much as the strength. Fully engaging with the challenges we experience can deepen our sense of purpose, reaffirm our values, and fortify our character. To build resilient character, we must embrace vulnerability, courage, and faith, faith in ourselves, in our values, and in our potential to overcome adversity.

Moreover, stories of resilience often reveal another profound truth: the power of giving back. When we unite our resilience with a commitment to uplifting others, we create a ripple effect. The character we build through our challenges can inspire and empower those around us. As we navigate our evolution and uphold our principles, our journeys can serve as blueprints for others who may find themselves facing similar adversities.

Consider the life of Malala Yousafzai, who, despite an assassination attempt for her advocacy of girls' education, emerged even more determined to fight for educational equity. Malala not only upheld her values in the face of extreme danger but also transformed her experience into a powerful platform for change. Her resilience redefined the conversation around access to education, empowering countless others to advocate for themselves and their communities.

Every individual possesses the potential to build a resilient character, yet the path will vary from person to person. It starts with honouring our values and recognising the moments when they are tested. When we find ourselves grappling with ethical dilemmas or choosing between convenience and principle, we must remember that we have the power to choose.

As we reflect on our values and consider how they endure through life's complexities, it is also beneficial to visualise the person we aspire to become. Imagine the character traits we admire and aspire to embody. What does resilience look like in our daily lives? What choices can we make to honour our values, even when it is challenging? Building a vision allows us to set actionable goals aligned with the person we want to become, guiding our efforts and decisions as we navigate adversity.

Moreover, cultivating a resilient character requires patience and perseverance. It is important to recognise that growth takes time. Each moment of vulnerability, each opportunity to choose integrity over ease, builds a foundation for our character over time. Resilience is not about avoiding difficulty; it is about rising and learning from each experience, softening the blows of hardship with the strength we acquire along the way.

To enhance our resilience, we can enlist strategies that enrich our lives, focusing on aspects such as:

Mindfulness: practising mindfulness allows us to cultivate awareness of our thoughts, emotions, and behaviours.

Goal setting: establishing clear, achievable goals aligned with our values provides direction.

Celebrating small victories: acknowledging and celebrating our progress, no matter how small, instils a sense of accomplishment.

Seeking mentorship: surrounding ourselves with mentors or role models who exemplify resilient character can inspire us. They can provide guidance, wisdom, and encouragement, reminding us that we are not alone in our struggles.

The path toward building a resilient character is one woven with stories of individuals who, through commitment to their principles, have shaped their lives and the lives of others. Each narrative inspires us to reflect on our own values and the strength required to stay true to them amidst the storms we face.

As you embark on your journey of self-discovery and character building, allow yourself to be guided by the stories of resilience before you. Embrace the challenges as opportunities for growth; let your values become your compass, leading you through uncharted territories. Forge connections with those who uplift and support you, and remain committed to practising self-awareness, adaptability, and integrity.

By cultivating a resilient character, you empower yourself not only to overcome adversity but also to inspire those around you to do the same. Just as the journey of becoming is ongoing, so too is the process of resilience, a powerful companion in the pursuit of your best self. Stand firm in your convictions, embrace your challenges, and step boldly into the future with the strength of character that will guide you on your way.

The Courage to Stand Alone

In the intricate tapestry of life, we often find ourselves at crossroads where the choices we make become reflections of our character. One of the most challenging yet gratifying paths is the courage to uphold our personal values, especially when those values stand in contrast to prevailing opinions or societal norms. This courage is not merely a trait but a testament to the strength of character that defines who we are.

Standing firm in one's beliefs can be a solitary endeavour. The pressure to conform looms large, often swaying even the most resolute hearts. It demands an unwavering commitment to authenticity and integrity, qualities that are vital for anyone who aspires to live a life of significance rather than a life marked solely by success. In this subchapter, we explore the immense worth of maintaining personal values during turbulent times, the inner resolve required to navigate solitude, and the profound insights gained from periods of introspection.

To begin, we must acknowledge that each of us possesses a unique moral compass, an internal guide that informs our decisions, influences our actions, and shapes our interactions with others. This compass is embedded in our values, informed by a confluence of experiences, culture, upbringing, and personal reflections. However, the journey to discovering and embracing these values is often fraught with challenges. It requires self-examination, courage, and a willingness to face the discomfort that accompanies standing apart from the crowd.

The first step in cultivating this courage is fostering deep self-awareness. Understanding what we stand for is pivotal not only in guiding our actions but also in fortifying our resolve when faced with dissent. Self-awareness requires us to confront our beliefs honestly, separating them from societal expectations and external influences. It calls for quiet moments of reflection, where we can sift through the noise and uncover what truly resonates with our values.

Consider the moments in your life when you felt compelled to conform. Perhaps it was a time at work when everyone endorsed a questionable business practice, or a social gathering where opinions aligned with popular sentiment, leaving you feeling out of sync. In those instances, the tension between maintaining your integrity and yielding to collective pressure can be palpable. Standing alone in such moments can feel daunting, yet it is precisely in these moments that character is both tested and refined.

Courage is an essential part of this process. It is not the absence of fear but the resolve to act despite it. By acknowledging our fears around isolation and judgment, we develop a deeper understanding of what is at stake when we choose to stand firm. We often fear the solitude that may accompany authenticity, yet solitude can serve as fertile ground for growth. In moments of solitude, we can delve deeper into our values, clarify our thoughts, and gather strength from within.

The experience of standing alone is often depicted as isolating, yet it can also be profoundly empowering. Many influential figures have walked this path: Gandhi, Martin Luther King Jr., and Malala Yousafzai, to name a few. Each faced isolation and resistance, yet persevered by remaining true to their beliefs. Their legacies remind us that courage can illuminate the darkness of solitude, transforming it into a source of strength. Their narratives speak to the enduring impact of a character forged in adversity.

While solitude can be uncomfortable, it offers an invaluable opportunity for introspection and self-discovery. In the quiet, away from the cacophony of external influences, we can hear our thoughts more clearly. We can confront fears, acknowledge weaknesses, and celebrate strengths without the noise of others dulling our perceptions. Through this reflection, we distil our values, reinforcing our commitment to uphold them even when the world seems intent on leading us astray.

Another critical aspect of standing alone is recognising that not everyone will understand or support our values. In a world that often prioritises conformity, being true to oneself can be met with scepticism or even hostility. This reality necessitates a strong foundation of self-confidence and conviction. It requires being ready to explain and advocate for our values, even in the face of opposition. The ability to articulate our beliefs with clarity and confidence is essential. It allows us to engage in meaningful discussions, asserting the integrity of our stance without succumbing to defensiveness or aggression.

Relationships are essential to our well-being, but the quality of those relationships must align with our values. When we remain true to ourselves, we naturally attract people who resonate with our perspectives and support our journey. Conversely, maintaining relationships that undermine our beliefs can lead to internal conflict, dissatisfaction, and emotional strain. It is vital to examine our relationships through the lens of our values, recognising those that uplift us and distancing ourselves from those that hinder our growth.

Standing firm in one's beliefs does not imply rigid rejection of opposing views. Rather, it opens the door to constructive dialogue, allowing us to approach differences with respect and curiosity. True strength lies not only in unwavering adherence to one's stance but also in the willingness to listen, learn, and evolve. Engaging with contrasting perspectives can deepen our understanding and refine our values further.

To cultivate this courage, we can use practical strategies. One powerful tool is journaling. It enables us to articulate our beliefs, reflect on experiences, and document our evolution. Writing offers a sacred space for exploration, helping to clarify feelings, reconcile contradictions, and reinforce our commitments. It becomes a form of self-therapy that deepens self-awareness and enhances our understanding of our moral compass.

Additionally, surrounding ourselves with like-minded individuals can create a supportive community that encourages authenticity. Joining groups focused on personal development or values-based initiatives, or participating in online forums, can reinforce our commitment to our beliefs. By sharing our journeys with others who understand the struggle, we create spaces where courage is nurtured and solitude becomes more manageable.

Embracing vulnerability can be transformative. Admitting fears, uncertainties, or moments of doubt does not diminish our strength; instead, it humanises our experience. Vulnerability fosters deeper connections based on authenticity and mutual respect. When we share our journeys, complete with struggles and triumphs, we inspire others to find the courage to stand alone when necessary.

As we navigate the challenges of standing alone, it is essential to celebrate victories both large and small. Each moment we choose to act in accordance with our values, despite the risks, fortifies our character. Recognising these milestones boosts morale and reminds us of our strength and resolve.

Finally, we should acknowledge that the courage to stand alone is not static. It is an ongoing journey. As we evolve and grow, our values may shift, prompting us to revisit and reassess what we stand for. This fluidity requires an open mind and open heart, affirming that staying true to oneself also means being open to change. In doing so, we cultivate resilience and adaptability, essential qualities in an ever-changing world.

In conclusion, the courage to stand alone is a defining feature of strong character. It transcends the mere acceptance of one's beliefs; it encompasses living authentically, embracing solitude as a source of strength, and engaging thoughtfully with the world around us. This journey is not easy, but it is in the struggle that we discover the depths of our character and the significance of our unique contributions.

By fostering self-awareness, embracing solitude, cultivating vulnerability, and reaffirming our values, we not only navigate the challenges of standing alone but also empower ourselves to become the architects of our destinies. This courage is a guiding light in our journey of becoming, the essence of what it means to strive for our best selves. As we learn to be true to ourselves amid external pressures, we not only experience profound personal growth but also inspire others to embark on their own journeys of authenticity.

Relationships and Influence

The Tapestry of Human Connection

The journey of personal growth is often profoundly shaped by the tapestry of human connections we weave throughout our lives. Our relationships serve as a crucial framework for constructing our identities, beliefs, and aspirations. They act as mirrors, reflecting our strengths and weaknesses and guiding us toward self-discovery and greater self-awareness.

As we navigate our paths, the impact of those we choose to surround ourselves with becomes increasingly significant. The supportive relationships we cultivate can act as a catalyst for positive change, pushing us toward our potential, while toxic or unsupportive connections can impede our growth.

In this exploration of the tapestry of human connection, we will delve into the various dimensions of relationships and their transformative power, examining how our social networks affect our journeys of becoming.

When considering the influence of relationships on personal development, it is essential to recognise that we are inherently social beings. The support systems we create and maintain provide not only emotional and psychological sustenance but also offer tangible benefits in terms of accountability and encouragement. Positive connections can propel us forward in our pursuits, fostering an environment where we can thrive. Conversely, negative connections can stifle our progress, leaving us feeling isolated, unmotivated, or misunderstood.

The Power of Becoming

The impact of social networks on our personal transformation is profound and multifaceted. Studies reveal that individuals with strong social networks experience increased longevity, improved mental health, and heightened resilience when facing life's challenges. Furthermore, these connections provide opportunities for learning, modelling behaviours, and receiving feedback that enhances personal growth. Within the fabric of human interaction, those who surround us play an instrumental role in shaping our beliefs, attitudes, and ultimately our actions.

To appreciate the significance of supportive relationships in personal growth, consider the role of mentorship. Mentors are individuals who guide and elevate our experiences, offering wisdom gleaned from their own journeys. The relationship between a mentor and mentee is a powerful conduit for learning, where knowledge is shared and growth is nurtured. A mentor can provide invaluable insights that help us recognise and harness our strengths while encouraging us to confront our weaknesses. This dynamic illustrates how interconnectedness can enrich our lives, guiding us to see possibilities we might never have identified on our own.

Additionally, our peers profoundly influence our growth. The adage, "You are the average of the five people you spend the most time with," is a striking reminder of the power of association. Friends and colleagues who embody positive traits, such as ambition, kindness, and resilience, can inspire and motivate us to embody similar qualities. Social contagion theory suggests that behaviours, attitudes, and even emotions can spread through social networks, reinforcing the idea that who we surround ourselves with directly impacts our journey toward our best selves.

The Power of Becoming

Building these positive networks requires intention and vulnerability. To form meaningful connections, one must be willing to share authentic parts of oneself, creating an environment where trust can flourish. This openness allows for deeper conversations and understanding, paving the way for transformative experiences. An authentic relationship thrives on mutual vulnerability, where both parties feel safe to express their thoughts, fears, and aspirations. This dynamic can be particularly influential in moments of uncertainty or self-doubt, as having a supportive voice can provide the encouragement needed to take the following steps.

Another facet of human connection is the impact of shared experiences. Engaging in activities or projects with others can foster camaraderie, as shared experiences often deepen relationships. Whether it is collaborating on a work project, participating in a community service initiative, or simply enjoying a hobby together, these shared moments create treasured memories that serve as anchors in our relationships. Through challenges faced together and triumphs celebrated in unison, individuals can forge bonds that reinforce their commitment to one another and their growth.

One cannot discuss the tapestry of human connection without examining the role of family. Family relationships can significantly shape our values, self-perception, and interpersonal skills. The foundational experiences we have with family members influence our comfort with vulnerability, our communication styles, and our ability to form connections outside the familial sphere. Families can be sources of immense support, providing a nurturing environment conducive to exploration and growth. However, family dynamics are not always supportive, and toxic relationships within families can hinder personal development. Recognising these patterns is crucial for breaking free from limiting beliefs and fostering healthier connections.

While some relationships inherently provide the support we need, others may require boundaries to prevent our growth from being stifled. Establishing these boundaries is a vital skill in navigating relationships, allowing individuals to prioritise their well-being while maintaining connections with others. A boundary can serve as a protective mechanism, ensuring that the influence of others does not overwhelm us or lead us down paths that compromise our values or aspirations. Communicating these boundaries clearly can foster mutual respect and understanding, helping to cultivate relationships that contribute positively to our journeys.

The stories of those who have experienced profound transformations through their connections illustrate the potency of human relationships. Consider individuals who have found success through the encouragement of a friend or family member who believed in their potential when they did not. Many entrepreneurs credit their peers' inspiration and support for taking the leap into the unknown and pursuing their dreams. These narratives remind us that our connections, be they familial, platonic, or professional, can provide the scaffolding we need to build our lives.

The tapestry of human connection extends beyond our immediate circle, also encompassing broader social networks. In our increasingly digital world, the nature of connection has evolved, leading to relationships that span geographical boundaries and cultural differences. Social media platforms provide a means to connect with others who share our interests or experiences, fostering communities where individuals can support one another. Although online interactions can sometimes feel less personal, they can still cultivate significant relationships that enrich our lives.

However, it is essential to approach digital connections mindfully. While the convenience of connecting with others online is remarkable, it is crucial to balance these interactions with genuine face-to-face connections. Virtual relationships can bolster our networks, but they should not replace the depth and intimacy often cultivated in person. Striving for a balance between both can create a well-rounded support system that nourishes our growth.

In the age of information, the importance of discernment within our networks cannot be overstated. Surrounding ourselves with those who share our values and uplift our aspirations requires a conscious effort to assess the influence of each relationship on our lives. It can be tempting to prioritise quantity over quality in our connections, but the depth of a relationship often holds far more significance than the number of acquaintances we maintain. By cultivating a circle of support composed of individuals who challenge, inspire, and encourage our growth, we harness the full potential of human connection.

While the tapestry of human connection is richly woven, it is also essential to acknowledge that relationships evolve. People change, circumstances shift, and sometimes connections fade. Recognising when a relationship is no longer conducive to our growth allows us to make intentional choices about our social networks. This can be a challenging process, tinged with emotional complexity, but it is part of the journey of becoming. Just as we should seek out connections that uplift us, we must also be willing to let go of those that impede our progress.

The Power of Becoming

Embracing the ebb and flow of relationships creates the space to invite new connections into our lives. Each interaction brings new possibilities for growth, learning, and collaboration. The tapestry of our lives is continually woven with threads of different colours and textures, each relationship contributing to the overall design. Embracing this fluidity helps us become more adaptable and open, allowing us to flourish as we encounter new experiences and perspectives.

In conclusion, the tapestry of human connection is a vital aspect of our personal growth. Our relationships are not mere accessories in our journey; they are fundamental to the very fabric of who we are and who we aspire to become. Through supportive connections, we gain insight, encouragement, and strength that propel us forward. We learn to navigate the complexities of character and emotions, grounding ourselves in the presence of others who share our values and dreams. As we cultivate these relationships with intentionality and authenticity, we create a supportive network that serves as a springboard for our transformation.

The interconnectedness of our lives reminds us that we do not journey alone. Every interaction offers an opportunity for mutual growth, highlighting the importance of nurturing relationships that enhance our experiences. As we become more mindful of the influence of our social networks, we empower ourselves to engage with others in meaningful ways, ultimately contributing to a richer, more fulfilling journey of becoming. Moving forward, let us embrace the power of these relationships, recognising their role in shaping our best selves as we weave our own unique tapestries of human connection.

Setting Healthy Boundaries in Relationships

In our journey toward becoming our best selves, the relationships we cultivate play a significant role in shaping our experiences and growth. The connections we nurture with family, friends, colleagues, and communities can elevate us, inspire us, and support our aspirations. However, these relationships demand a delicate balance between the love and support we give and the independence we must maintain. Setting healthy boundaries is crucial in ensuring that our relationships are not only beneficial but also nurturing for our own personal growth.

Defining what healthy boundaries look like in relationships begins with understanding the nature of boundaries themselves. Boundaries are not walls that separate us from others; they are flexible lines that define where one individual ends and another begins. They serve as guidelines that help us protect our emotional and physical well-being, allowing us to engage in relationships that are sustainable and mutually beneficial. Healthy boundaries enhance our relationships by fostering respect, understanding, and cooperation.

At times, the line between support and sacrifice can blur, leading to feelings of resentment, burnout, or frustration. It is vital to recognise that setting boundaries is an act of self-care and a demonstration of self-respect. Boundaries inform others of our limits and needs, allowing us to communicate effectively and maintain our independence, even in the closest relationships. This becomes especially important as we strive to honour our individual paths while still engaging with those we cherish.

To cultivate healthy boundaries, the first step is self-reflection. Understanding your own needs, values, and feelings is vital in defining what you expect from others and what you are willing to give. Take time to reflect on past experiences where boundaries were tested. Ask yourself questions such as: When did I feel overwhelmed? What made me feel valued or disrespected? Were there moments when I said "yes" out of obligation rather than genuine desire? These inquiries can illuminate patterns that help you identify specific boundary issues in your current relationships that need addressing.

Communicating our needs can often feel daunting, but it is a crucial component of boundary setting. One effective method is to approach conversations with honesty and openness, expressing how certain behaviours affect you personally. Use "I" statements to convey your feelings without projecting blame onto others. For example, instead of saying, "You always interrupt me," you might say, "I feel unheard when I am interrupted." This shift in language encourages dialogue and minimises defensiveness, creating space for constructive conversation.

Active listening is equally essential in these discussions. Once you express your needs, invite the other person to share their thoughts. Demonstrating that you are willing to consider their perspective can foster mutual understanding and respect. Approach the conversation as a cooperative endeavour rather than a confrontation. It is vital that both parties feel valued and understood, creating an environment conducive to setting and respecting boundaries.

However, not all discussions about boundaries will go smoothly. Conflicts may arise when others resist your efforts to assert your needs. Understanding the potential for conflict can help you navigate tough conversations. When faced with resistance or confrontation, practise staying calm and maintaining your composure. Take a step back if needed, allowing emotions to settle before continuing the dialogue. Remember that the goal is not to win the argument but to reach a mutual understanding that honours both your boundaries and the other person's feelings.

It is also essential to recognise that boundaries are not static; they can shift as relationships evolve. Periodically reassess your boundaries, ensuring they still align with your personal growth and desires. Initiating these conversations periodically can help clear up misunderstandings and reinforce the importance of mutual respect. Being willing to adapt promotes healthy communication practices that strengthen relationships.

Establishing boundaries is not just about communicating your own needs; it is about acknowledging and respecting others' boundaries as well. Healthy relationships are based on reciprocity, where both individuals honour each other's limits. This mutual respect creates a strong foundation that allows both parties to thrive without feelings of guilt, obligation, or resentment. When we honour others' boundaries, we signal that their autonomy is valued, which further encourages openness and trust.

Forging healthy boundaries can also help in curbing feelings of guilt or obligation. Many individuals struggle with saying "no," fearing it may damage a relationship or disappoint someone they care about. However, saying "no" when it is necessary is a significant part of maintaining your well-being. Practising self-compassion will help you understand that prioritising your needs is not selfish; rather, it is an essential step in becoming your best self.

A relationship built on giving at the expense of your own needs is unsustainable and undermines your growth journey.

Setting boundaries can require a shift in mindset, particularly in societies that encourage prioritising harmony and relationships over individual needs. Challenge any thoughts that suggest it is wrong to put yourself first. Embracing your right to set boundaries empowers you to cultivate relationships that support your journey and allow others to flourish as well.

Engaging in personal growth often entails surrounding ourselves with positive influences that uplift us. Part of this process requires being selective about the individuals whose energy and presence we invite into our lives. Identifying unhealthy dynamics in relationships, such as those that drain our energy, belittle our ambitions, or create an atmosphere of negativity, is vital. Setting effective boundaries may mean distancing ourselves from these toxic influences or being firm in our resolve not to engage in detrimental conversations or behaviours.

The importance of maintaining balance extends into our professional relationships as well. In a workplace setting, it can be challenging to assert boundaries due to the hierarchical nature of many organisations. However, establishing clear boundaries at work can enhance both our productivity and our job satisfaction. This might involve setting limits on after-hours availability, communicating expectations regarding workload, or addressing inappropriate interactions or unsolicited advice.

Conflict may arise in professional relationships when setting boundaries, especially if others are accustomed to a different dynamic. Here, applying the same principles of open communication, self-reflection, and active listening is paramount. Your value in the workplace is defined not by your willingness to overextend yourself but by your unique contributions, talents, and perspective. Upholding your boundaries cultivates respect and can lead to more profound professional relationships.

Another aspect of boundaries in relationships is recognising the emotional toll of overextending yourself. Many people fall into the pattern of feeling obliged to help everyone, often at their own expense. This caretaker role can become exhausting and counterproductive. Acknowledging the importance of self-care is integral in preventing burnout and enabling you to be fully present in your relationships.

Setting healthy boundaries offers us the opportunity to build deeper connections based on authenticity and transparency. When we assert our needs, it often inspires others to do the same. This openness can foster a shared understanding and create an atmosphere where both partners feel empowered to express their vulnerabilities, thereby increasing the intimacy and emotional depth of the relationship.

Moreover, boundaries serve to clarify expectations. Ensuring you and your partner understand what is acceptable and what is not can prevent misunderstandings and enhance trust. Clarity in communication reduces the risk of friction and enables both individuals to navigate the relationship with confidence.

One must also consider the potential impact of external influences on personal boundaries. Societal norms, cultural expectations, and family influences can intertwine to form a backdrop against which relationships are assessed and understood.

These influences can complicate boundary-setting, as one may feel pressure to conform to certain roles or expectations. Take a personal inventory of these influences and examine how they shape your views on relationships and assertiveness. Identifying societal pressures and challenging them can empower you to establish boundaries that feel right for you.

As difficult as it may feel at times, cultivating the ability to assert ourselves is a significant act of self-love. It reflects a commitment to honouring our individuality in the context of relationships. While it may feel uncomfortable initially, practice will help ease the process. The more we assert our boundaries, the more natural this self-advocacy will become.

Furthermore, revisiting the concept of empathy can enhance our boundary-setting efforts. Empathy allows us to connect deeply with others and understand their responses to our boundary-setting. Cultivating empathy fosters compassion, making it easier to recognise when others are struggling to understand or respect your boundaries. This understanding can also help ease any feelings of conflict or discomfort that may arise during these conversations.

As we delve deeper into our own emotional landscapes, we become more adept at recognising and asserting our limits. Embracing our vulnerability enables us to have more authentic conversations about our needs and values. This emotional honesty enhances our capacity for connection, creating healthier dynamics in our relationships.

In conclusion, setting healthy boundaries in relationships is a vital skill essential for our growth and overall well-being. It allows us to engage authentically with others while honouring our individual needs. Through self-reflection, effective communication, mutual respect, and a commitment to our own growth, we can foster connections that empower us and those around us. Establishing boundaries is not merely about protecting ourselves; it is about creating a foundation for genuine relationships to thrive.

As you continue on your journey to becoming your best self, remember that healthy boundaries are essential for nurturing positive relationships. Engage in conversations that clarify needs, address conflicts constructively, and emphasise respect for both your individuality and others' autonomy. Embrace the power of boundaries and watch as your relationships flourish, propelling you toward your most authentic self.

Surrounding Yourself with Positivity

As we navigate the journey of becoming our best selves, one undeniable truth stands out: the people we surround ourselves with can significantly shape our path. Just as iron sharpens iron, the company we keep can elevate us or hold us back. This subchapter emphasises the importance of surrounding oneself with uplifting individuals who foster our growth and well-being. It is not merely about having friends; it is about creating a support network that encourages, empowers, and enlightens.

To understand how to surround ourselves with positivity, we must first acknowledge what this entails. Positive relationships are characterised by mutual respect, encouragement, and a genuine interest in each other's growth. Those we allow into our innermost circles can either uplift us through their support and empowerment or drain us with negativity and scepticism. Therefore, the intentional selection of our social connections becomes paramount.

The Power of Becoming

A supportive network does not merely consist of friends and family who are always agreeable and complimentary. Instead, it comprises individuals who challenge us to stretch beyond our comfort zones, who believe in our potential even when we doubt ourselves, and who provide honest feedback conducive to our personal development. In this pursuit, it is vital to distinguish between those who are supportive and those who merely tolerate us, for the former contribute to our flourishing while the latter can compromise our journey of becoming.

In contemplating my own relationships, I recall a period in my life when I was surrounded by a group of friends who, although well-meaning, were steeped in negativity. Our conversations often revolved around complaints about work, disillusionment with personal goals, and a habitual focus on what was lacking in our lives. Energy that could have been spent on constructive planning for our dreams was instead siphoned into cycles of negativity.

I vividly remember one particular gathering where a friend shared an idea she had been nurturing for years, her dream of starting a business. Instead of buoying her spirit, most of the group responded with grumbles about potential barriers and scepticism about her ability to succeed. In that moment, the weight of those words not only crushed her spirit but also revealed how easily negativity can infiltrate our lives.

Recognising the detrimental impact of my social circle was a pivotal realisation. It propelled me to assess my relationships critically, identifying who in my life possessed genuine enthusiasm for growth, a thirst for positivity, and a belief in dreaming big. Subsequently, I chose to invest my time and energy in nurturing relationships with individuals who were not only positive but also proactive, people who sought to propel themselves and others forward.

One of the most empowering strategies for fostering enriching relationships is cultivating awareness of our own energy. Just as we absorb the energies of those around us, we also emit an energy that influences our interactions. Environments with vibrant positivity often breed constructive conversations, laughter, and hope. When we become beacons of positivity in our circles, we inadvertently attract like-minded individuals who seek the same uplifting presence in their lives. Thus, our transformation is not solely about seeking positivity in others but also about embodying those traits ourselves.

Another effective strategy is to practise gratitude in our relationships. Regularly acknowledging what we appreciate in our friends can deepen connections and foster a rich atmosphere of positivity. Simple acts of appreciation, whether through a heartfelt message, a thoughtful gesture, or simply sharing what a friend means to us, can elevate the quality of our interactions. By focusing on gratitude, we begin to shift our mindset from one of scarcity, fearing we are not enough or that our relationships will falter, to one of abundance, recognising the value each person adds to our lives.

As I cultivated relationships with individuals who challenged me to grow, I encountered a mentor who reshaped my perception of positivity. She was a rarity, an individual who radiated optimism yet possessed a grounded understanding of life's challenges. During our discussions, she would draw on her own experiences of setbacks and triumphs, sharing stories of resilience that encouraged me to embrace my own struggles.

The Power of Becoming

In a particularly difficult phase of my career, she noted, "Success is not a straight line. It is a jagged path filled with lessons, and it is those lessons that shape us." This perspective was revolutionary. It reframed failure from being something to be feared into a stepping stone toward authentic growth. In turn, I found myself seeking out other relationships where this duality of positivity and realism thrived.

To create a positive support system, consider the following strategies:

1. Be Intentional About Your Connections

Evaluate the people around you. Who inspires you? Who listens and offers constructive feedback rather than dismissive comments? List the individuals who exhibit the traits you admire and aspire to cultivate within yourself. Aim to maintain connections with those individuals while gradually distancing yourself from sources of negativity.

2. Engage in Open and Honest Communication

Positivity thrives in environments that encourage open communication. Share your struggles and aspirations candidly and invite your friends to do the same. By embracing vulnerability, you create a safe space for authentic conversations that bolster mutual growth.

3. Set Boundaries

In nurturing a positive circle, recognise the importance of setting boundaries. It is vital to create distance from relationships that drain your energy, cause undue stress, or foster constant negativity. This might mean having difficult conversations or limiting interactions with individuals who do not contribute positively to your life.

4. Cultivate Mutual Growth

Seek friendships based on shared interests and aspirations. Whether it is starting a book club, participating in community service, or joining hobbyist groups, actively seek opportunities to spend time with those who inspire you. When you engage in shared activities that promote growth, your relationships deepen, and you cultivate an environment rich with positivity.

5. Invest Time and Energy

Talent and drive often flourish in environments where time and effort are dedicated to nurturing connections. Make an intentional effort to reach out, check on friends, and invest in relationships. This not only strengthens bonds but also reinforces a network grounded in positivity.

6. Become a Source of Positivity

Consider how you can elevate the energy in your relationships. Be a force that inspires others by practising kindness, resilience, and a growth mindset yourself. Slow down and offer assistance, be generous with compliments, and share encouraging words.

The Power of Becoming

One personal anecdote resonates vividly with these strategies. After a particularly challenging year marked by career changes and personal losses, I made a conscious choice to cultivate relationships with those who shared a vision of success and positivity. During weekly meet-ups with a small accountability group, we shared not only our goals but also our challenges. In one gathering, I confessed my moments of self-doubt regarding a project that I had long dreamed of establishing. As I shared my fears, rather than mere sympathy, my friends responded with encouragement, tangible ideas for overcoming obstacles, and shared their own messy journeys in pursuit of their dreams. This collective positive energy propelled me forward, motivating me to confront my fears and embrace them as part of the process of becoming.

Moreover, positively influencing others can be an incredible aspect of our growth journey. When we actively contribute to the uplifting of others, we often find ourselves enriched in the process. This reciprocity nurtures our relationships, creating a cycle of encouraging growth and support. One of my closest friends, whom I have known for over a decade, has encouraged me not only through her advice but also through her actions. She regularly volunteers for causes close to her heart and brings a sense of passion and positivity into challenging situations.

Watching her navigate these intricate paths of life with grace has inspired me to step out of my comfort zone as well. In turn, I have tried to support her ambitions with both enthusiasm and constructive insights, creating an atmosphere of mutual growth and support.

Reflecting on these experiences leads to an invaluable realisation: our circles reflect ourselves. They mirror our aspirations, beliefs, and attitudes. Through cultivating positivity and fostering uplifting relationships, we open ourselves to transformational growth.

Therefore, I encourage you to take a moment and assess your own circles. Consider who fills your emotional reservoir and who drains it. Reflect on the potential of your relationships to empower you on your journey of becoming.

The influence of our social circles is not to be taken lightly. These interactions nurture our dreams, ground our ideas, and shape our character. Embarking on the journey of becoming your best self is undoubtedly personal, yet the company you keep plays an integral role in this transformation. The strength of your relationships can push you beyond your perceived limits, buoying you through disappointments and celebrating your victories.

As you take this journey, remind yourself that cultivating a positive support network is not a task completed in haste. It is a continual process of nurturing relationships, building appreciation habits, and fostering healthy communication. Surrounding yourself with positivity not only enriches your life but also allows you to bloom in ways you might never have envisioned.

Today, reflect on your current network. Who are the uplifting individuals you can invest more time in? How can you enhance the positive spirit in your relationships? Embrace this journey wholeheartedly and watch the profound changes unfold in your life. Becoming your best self is a shared journey, and the positivity of your support network can illuminate the path forward.

The Courage to Fail Forward

Redefining Failure

In our fast-paced, results-oriented society, failure is often viewed as a dirty word, a stigma that invokes feelings of shame, inadequacy, and defeat. We are conditioned from an early age to chase success relentlessly, celebrating only the winners and overlooking the many paths strewn with mistakes that provide the contour of our lives.

This all-consuming pursuit of success often renders failure an enemy to be avoided at all costs. We hear mantras like "failure is not an option" splashed across motivational posters and invoked in speeches, implying that to fail is to fall short in a way that defines our entire worth. However, this detrimental perspective can stifle our natural drive for growth and transformation.

Instead of merely avoiding failure, it is essential to redefine what it means. Failure, if we allow it, can be a powerful teacher, a stepping stone toward personal evolution. It provides insight, builds resilience, and fosters the courage needed to take future risks. To reframe our understanding of failure, we need to explore the societal narratives that shape our perceptions and examine how we can shift our mindset to embrace failure as an inevitable part of life.

One of the crucial steps in redefining failure is to recognise that society often glorifies success without acknowledging the myriad failures that precede it. The stories we hear about great entrepreneurs, scientists, and artists always highlight their significant accomplishments but frequently gloss over the numerous attempts and missteps that were part of their journeys.

The Power of Becoming

For instance, Thomas Edison famously said, "I have not failed. I have just found 10,000 ways that will not work." Yet how many children grow up believing that taking risks is the path to success when they have been taught that failure is something to dread?

Reframing failure begins with recognising that it is not the opposite of success; it is part and parcel of the journey. Embracing a new narrative involves engaging with failure constructively, which can ultimately lead to deeper learning and a stronger foundation for future endeavours.

This perspective aligns with Carol Dweck's research on mindset, which distinguishes between a fixed mindset, in which individuals perceive their abilities and intelligence as static, and a growth mindset, which emphasises the belief that these can be developed. Those who adopt a growth mindset view challenges and setbacks as opportunities to learn rather than insurmountable barriers.

An illustrative piece of research conducted by Dr Andrew C Martin demonstrated that students who perceive obstacles, including failure, as development opportunities are more resilient and more likely to find creative solutions. His studies revealed that students with this growth-oriented approach performed better academically over time. Thus, finding courage in failure does not merely consist of internalising setbacks but leveraging them as tools for progress.

Turning to personal stories illuminates the transformational power of redefined failure. Consider the narrative of J K Rowling, the author of the beloved Harry Potter series. Before her monumental success, Rowling faced numerous challenges, including rejection letters from publishers and personal struggles such as poverty and depression. Each setback could have easily labelled her a failure, but instead, creativity and resilience became her tools for survival.

Rowling's journey exemplifies how those initial setbacks fuelled a more profound understanding of herself, her craft, and ultimately the heart of her story. When she finally published her first book, it became a cultural phenomenon that inspired millions and forever changed the literary landscape. She perceives her past failures as integral components of her path to success, demonstrating the courage to fail forward through every obstacle.

To provide further evidence of this idea, we can explore the distinction between failures of omission and failures of commission. Failures of omission refer to opportunities we miss by not taking action, while failures of commission arise when we attempt something that does not pan out as expected. Research in psychology shows that the pain of regretting missed opportunities often weighs more heavily than the discomfort of trying and failing.

When we carry the weight of unrealised potential on our shoulders, it illustrates the profound risk of not daring to pursue our ideas or dreams simply because we fear failure. Conversely, failures of commission, the initiatives we take on despite risks, can guide us toward self-discovery, deeper insight, and eventual achievement.

Daring to take action, even in the face of potential failure, often comes paired with significant learning. This concept is best illustrated in the realm of innovation. When companies like Google and Apple innovate, they do not shy away from risk; they embrace failure as part of the creative process. Projects like Google Glass or the Apple Maps launch show that even giants face obstacles.

However, rather than punishing themselves, they adopt iterative systems in which ideas are refined through feedback and failures, leading to more outstanding and inventive outcomes over time.

To fully embrace failure as an ally on our journeys, we must understand the valuable information it provides. Each mistake offers us critical insights regarding our choices, actions, and internal beliefs. When we consider failure as feedback, it shifts our consciousness from regret to learning.

Structured reflection and journaling practices can facilitate this process. By documenting our thoughts and experiences following a setback, we can analyse what went wrong, which contributions were ineffective, and how we might adapt our future strategies. This practice helps cultivate a learning mindset that repositions failure within a framework of growth.

Moreover, emotional resilience plays a significant role in how we perceive failure and respond to it. Emotional intelligence is paramount for managing our reactions and preventing negative feelings of shame and fear from dictating our behaviours. Building emotional awareness and adapting our responses can facilitate a more constructive relationship with failure.

For instance, when we revert to self-critical thinking patterns after a setback, acknowledging these feelings without letting them dominate can allow space for a more balanced perspective. Training ourselves to recognise failure as simply one chapter in a lengthy story aligns with the broader narrative of becoming our best selves.

Alongside personal growth, the catalyst of community cannot be understated in fostering a healthy attitude towards failure.

The Power of Becoming

Surrounding ourselves with individuals who celebrate our courage to try, even when the outcomes are lacklustre, can mitigate the fear of defeat. Creating networks and relationships grounded in mutual support can transform how we engage with risk and failure. Seeking mentors who share their struggles and setbacks can illustrate that the road to success is rarely perfectly paved.

Community fosters a culture where failure is accepted rather than feared, allowing individuals to become more resilient and more willing to step out of their comfort zones.

As we journey through life, we must remember that success is not a straight path; it is rarely a linear trajectory characterised solely by victories. Each misstep presents the opportunity for reflection, adaptation, and growth. By recognising the nuances of failure, we can begin to create a personal philosophy that embraces our setbacks.

Approaching failures with curiosity rather than judgment enables us to gain insights that deepen our understanding of who we are and what we can achieve.

In conclusion, redefining failure is a transformative process that requires courage, a reframed mindset, and a willingness to embrace vulnerability. When we succeed in viewing failures through the lens of opportunity, we unlock a world of potential and growth. No longer do we view failure as a sign of defeat; instead, it becomes a powerful ally in our pursuit of self-improvement and authenticity.

The journey of becoming our best selves demands that we foster resilience in the face of setbacks and that we engage with life fully, ready to learn from every experience. The courageous ones among us will not shy away from failure; they will recognise it as part of life's intricate tapestry, woven with lessons that enrich our narrative. By creating a culture that celebrates the courage to fail forward, we can inspire ourselves and others to take risks, explore new paths, and ultimately realise our fullest potential.

The Power of Recovery

In the journey of personal and professional development, failure is often an unwelcome companion. Yet the most profound lessons lie not in our triumphs but in how we respond to our setbacks. The power of recovery, therefore, becomes a critical aspect of the process we call "becoming." It is through the act of bouncing back that we build resilience, fortify our character, and emerge stronger than we were before.

This subchapter will explore the concept of bouncing back post-failure and equip you with strategies to embrace recovery as an integral part of your growth journey.

Failure can shatter our self-esteem and instil a paralysing fear of trying again. But rather than a final verdict, failure offers us a unique opportunity for reflection and a catalyst for change.

Notable figures throughout history exemplify this power of recovery. Consider Thomas Edison, whose commitment to persistence and innovation led to the invention of the light bulb after thousands of unsuccessful attempts. Each failure was not a setback to him but a stepping stone toward illuminating the world. Edison's famous quote, "I have not failed. I have just found 10,000 ways that will not work," encapsulates the mindset needed for recovery. He understood that every misstep contributed to his ultimate success.

The Power of Becoming

J K Rowling, author of the beloved Harry Potter series, faced several rejections from publishers before seeing her work in print. Living on welfare and battling depression, she could have easily surrendered to despair. Instead, she channelled her struggles into the magic of her storytelling. Through her journey, Rowling demonstrated that failure can fuel creativity and that recovery can lead to unexpected successes. Her story reminds us that our struggles do not define us; rather, it is our resilience in the face of them that shapes our futures.

Recovery demands courage. It requires a willingness to confront uncomfortable emotions and reflect on both successes and failures. It often means surrendering the need for perfection and embracing the beauty in the imperfect process of learning.

This journey of recovery involves several steps, beginning with acknowledging and accepting our failures. In moments of failure, our immediate response might skew toward self-criticism or denial. However, practising self-compassion is the antidote. Compassion allows us to treat ourselves with kindness, to recognise that we are human and prone to mistakes. By accepting our failures, we empower ourselves to analyse what went wrong without the heavy weight of self-judgment.

After acknowledgement, the need to analyse arises. This process means digging deep into the reasons behind our failures and identifying patterns that may hinder our progress. Reflective practices such as journaling can facilitate this analysis. Writing about our experiences enables us to articulate thoughts that often remain unspoken. It provides a space to explore what we could have done differently and fosters an environment to celebrate the lessons learned. By articulating our failures and their lessons, we develop a healthier relationship with failure itself.

The next step in the recovery process is to embrace adaptability. Change is a constant in life, yet many of us resist it. The ability to pivot and explore new strategies can turn a setback into an opportunity. When faced with a failure, ask yourself: What can I learn from this? What new approach can I take? By reframing failure as a chance to reevaluate our goals and methods, we become more agile in our pursuits.

For instance, a business that fails to meet its projections may need to shift its market strategy or adapt its product offerings. This adaptability not only aids in recovery but also paves the way for innovation.

Ultimately, resilience enables us to withstand challenges and emerge from them. Building resilience entails cultivating a mindset that views obstacles as temporary barriers rather than permanent roadblocks. This perspective shift is foundational to successfully navigating the waters of recovery.

A key strategy for developing resilience is fostering a supportive community. Relationships steeped in encouragement can bolster our spirits during tough times. Sharing experiences with others who have faced similar setbacks can normalise failure and reinforce the notion that we are not alone. It is these connections that remind us that each failure is part of a shared human experience.

As we embark on the path of recovery, it is essential to foster a growth mindset. Carol Dweck's research distinguishes between a fixed mindset, in which individuals believe their abilities are static, and a growth mindset, which embraces the idea that skills and intelligence can be developed through effort and learning. Adopting a growth mindset helps us see challenges as opportunities for development rather than insurmountable obstacles. It encourages us to view setbacks as valuable experiences that contribute to our ongoing journey of becoming.

The power of recovery can also be amplified through storytelling. Engaging with the narratives of others who have triumphed over adversity can inspire and motivate us. These stories serve as potent reminders that recovery is not just an abstract concept; it is a lived experience.

Consider the athlete Michael Jordan, who was famously cut from his high school basketball team. Instead of giving up, he used this failure as motivation to hone his skills, ultimately becoming one of the greatest basketball players of all time. His story teaches us that rejection can be the impetus for resilience, igniting a fire within to improve and excel.

Moreover, sharing our own stories of failure and recovery can create a ripple effect in our communities. By narrating our experiences, we normalise the conversation around failure and recovery, encouraging others to embrace their challenges rather than hide from them. In this way, recovery becomes a communal journey, one in which we lift each other as we navigate our own paths to resilience.

As we forge ahead, remember that recovery is not a one-time event but an ongoing process. It requires patience and dedication, as well as a willingness to grow through both good and bad experiences. Embracing this continuous cycle of trying, failing, and

The Power of Becoming

recovering empowers us to move forward confidently. By integrating the lessons of each setback, we lay the groundwork for a more effective and enlightened approach to both our personal and professional lives.

To strengthen your recovery capacity, consider creating a personal recovery action plan. This plan might include a list of self-care strategies, such as exercise, meditation, or hobbies that bring joy. It may also involve setting realistic goals that help you track progress over time. Importantly, this plan should incorporate reflective exercises that encourage growth, including regular check-ins with yourself to assess how you are navigating setbacks and identifying triggers that may lead to future failures.

In drawing this subchapter to a close, remember that the power of recovery hinges on our ability to embrace our full range of human experiences. We cannot control the inevitability of failure, but we can control how we respond to it. Embracing recovery is about harnessing our inner strength, learning from our missteps, and rebuilding ourselves in the process. It is an essential part of the journey to becoming your best self.

As you move forward, challenge yourself to celebrate your journey, not just the victories but also the moments of adversity that have shaped you. Each step you take, each setback you encounter, and each lesson you learn is a testament to your resilience and determination. By embracing the power of recovery, you equip yourself with the tools necessary to navigate future challenges and emerge stronger than ever before.

Remember, becoming is not a destination but a continuous journey. Let every setback fuel your drive to move forward and remain open to the growth that lies ahead.

Creating a Culture of Learning

In a world that often prioritises results over the journey to achieve them, fostering a culture of learning becomes a vital component of growth, not just for individuals but for groups, organisations, and communities as a whole. When we cultivate an environment that encourages curiosity, experimentation, and open discussions about failures, we create a space where resilience can thrive. This subchapter explores how to build such a culture, emphasising the significance of a growth-oriented mindset and the practical steps necessary to encourage open dialogue about failures and celebrate the associated learnings.

Before we delve into the mechanics of creating a culture of learning, it is essential to understand the underpinnings of a growth-oriented mindset. This mindset, famously conceptualised by psychologist Carol Dweck, posits that abilities can be developed through dedication and hard work. In contrast to a fixed mindset, which holds that skills and intelligence are static traits, a growth mindset fosters an environment ripe for learning and resilience. When we approach challenges with the understanding that we can grow from them, we foster a greater willingness to take risks, both individually and collectively.

At its core, a culture of learning encourages individuals to view setbacks and failures not as endpoints but as stepping stones to growth. This perspective shifts the focus from merely achieving success to embracing the process of learning that accompanies failures. When we can discuss our missteps openly, we create an environment of trust where individuals feel safe to share their experiences without fear of repercussion or humiliation. Emphasising collective resilience becomes paramount in this context; it is about how we lean on one another and derive strength from the community when faced with challenges.

The first step in creating a culture of learning is to initiate open dialogue about failure. Sharing stories of setbacks and the lessons learned from them allows individuals to connect on a deeper level. In schools, workplaces, and social environments, establishing a norm that allows people to openly discuss their failures encourages vulnerability, which, in turn, fosters connection and empathy. Individuals need to feel that their experiences are valued, and sharing these experiences can help craft a narrative that everyone is on a similar journey of growth.

Encouraging open dialogue can begin with leadership. Leaders play an influential role in shaping the culture of any environment. They must model the behaviour they wish to see by sharing their own failures and insights. When leaders admit their shortcomings, they send a powerful message that vulnerability is not a weakness but a part of the learning process. By normalising failures, they pave the way for everyone else to do the same.

Moreover, creating forums for these discussions can further enhance the culture of learning. Regular meetings or safe spaces where individuals can share their experiences, whether in team huddles, during staff training sessions, or at community gatherings, can set the tone for openness. The goal is to encourage storytelling as an integral part of your culture, highlighting the importance of each person's journey. Sharing victories is important, but sharing failures and what we gained from them can be even more powerful.

Another effective approach is to integrate learning and growth into performance reviews or assessments. Instead of focusing solely on outcomes, evaluations can include discussions on the challenges faced and the lessons learned. This not only shifts the emphasis from a strictly results-oriented mindset to a more holistic view of growth but also reinforces the importance of learning within the community or organisation. By celebrating efforts and resilience rather than just achievements, we create a culture that values the journey as much as the destination.

In addition to facilitating conversations about failure, it is essential to celebrate the learnings that arise from those experiences. Celebration does not always have to be grandiose; it can be as simple as acknowledging a team member who took a risk and learned something valuable or highlighting the insights gained from a project that did not go as planned. Recognition can take various forms, such as shout-outs in meetings, inclusion in newsletters, or simple verbal affirmations. The key is to make celebrating the learning process a habitual practice.

This practice not only honours individual contributions but also reinforces the idea that learning is a communal effort. When successes are shared broadly and the lessons from failures are acknowledged, it cultivates a spirit of collaboration and support. The culture shifts from one of competition, where individuals feel they must outshine one another, to one where collective success is prioritised.

The Power of Becoming

Integrating learning into the fabric of a community involves developing systems that facilitate ongoing education and growth. Workshops, seminars, and training sessions that focus not only on skill development but also on handling failures and learning from them can enhance communal resilience. Creating spaces for continuous learning promotes adaptability and equips individuals with the tools they need to navigate challenges effectively. This is particularly important in fast-paced or innovative fields where change is the only constant.

Fostering a culture of learning also means recognising and addressing the barriers that hinder open dialogue about failure. Fear of judgment, repercussions, or negative consequences can stifle honest conversations and discourage individuals from sharing their experiences. To mitigate these fears, it is crucial to maintain a non-judgmental atmosphere where every contribution is received with respect and understanding. This requires ongoing work from everyone in the community, particularly leaders who set the tone.

Moreover, the power of language cannot be overlooked. The terminology used in discussions about failure matters significantly. Choosing words that are constructive rather than punitive can influence how individuals perceive their own experiences. Instead of framing a setback as a "failure," it can be recast as a "learning opportunity." This language change encourages individuals to view their experiences through a lens of possibility rather than limitation.

For a culture of learning to take hold, it must be woven into the very fabric of community relationships. This extends beyond formal structures and into everyday interactions and conversations. Practising active listening, asking thoughtful questions, and providing constructive feedback are ways to reinforce this culture in daily life. Building trust and showing that you value another person's input creates a solid foundation for open dialogues about growth and learning.

Encouraging risk-taking is another pivotal element in creating a culture of learning. When individuals are given the freedom to experiment, they discover new possibilities that may not have been evident within rigid structures. Encouraging creativity and innovation while supporting those who might fail allows people to reach their full potential. Leaders should explicitly invite individuals to take calculated risks and reassure them that failure is not only permissible but vital for progress.

Recognising and addressing the diversity of experiences within a community is also crucial for fostering a learning culture. Everyone comes with unique perspectives and backgrounds, which shape how they perceive and respond to failures. Approaching conversations with an understanding that different viewpoints exist ensures that all voices are included. This openness can lead to richer discussions and a more comprehensive understanding of the lessons that can be drawn from various failures.

As individuals begin to engage in open dialogues about failure and celebrate learnings, they will likely encounter resistance, either from within themselves or from others. It is important to anticipate such challenges and embrace them as opportunities for growth. Resistance might stem from deeply ingrained beliefs about failure, self-doubt, or fear of vulnerability. By addressing these emotions honestly and compassionately, communities can create an even stronger foundation for their culture of learning.

The Power of Becoming

Establishing mentorship programmes can be another powerful way to reinforce this culture. Mentorship creates a structured avenue for individuals to learn from one another's experiences, especially from failures. By providing opportunities for informed insights and guidance, organisations and communities can enhance their shared resilience. Mentors can share their own setbacks and how they turned those experiences into learning moments. Such shared stories amplify the community's understanding of growth through adversity.

Feedback mechanisms are also integral to establishing a culture of learning. Implementing anonymous surveys or suggestion boxes can allow individuals to voice their experiences and concerns about failures and growth without fear. This collected information can highlight common themes or challenges, guiding the community in understanding where additional support is needed. Creating a continuous feedback loop further cements the commitment to growth.

Supporting ongoing education through access to resources, whether books, seminars, or curated experiences, can enhance collective growth. Investing in training that specifically addresses setbacks, resilience, and personal development enriches the community's knowledge base. Whether through formal programmes or informal learning opportunities, providing avenues for education fosters an ever-evolving culture of learning.

As a final goal, integrating the principles of a learning culture into community values is paramount. These principles should transcend individual experiences and become part of the collective identity. When the community embraces learning as a fundamental value, it ensures that every member contributes to and nurtures this environment. Reinforcing values of curiosity, experimentation, and collaboration becomes part of the community's shared DNA.

To cultivate resilience through a culture of learning, you must recognise that it is an ongoing journey. Creating an environment where failure is viewed as an essential component of growth requires continuous effort and commitment from everyone involved. It necessitates a shift in mindset that values learning alongside achievement, one where triumphs are celebrated but lessons from failures are regarded just as highly.

In conclusion, creating a culture of learning is not just about discussing failures; it is about weaving a rich tapestry of experiences, insights, and growth that bind individuals together. By encouraging open dialogue, celebrating learnings, fostering mentorship, and instilling shared values, we can build communities that not only survive but thrive in the face of adversity. Through this collective journey of becoming, we empower one another to embrace the courage to fail forward, thus shaping environments that enhance resilience and foster lifelong learning.

Ultimately, the power of becoming is magnified when individuals within a community feel supported and empowered to learn from every experience, shaping a future full of growth opportunities.

Discovering Your Why

The Importance of Purpose

Finding one's purpose in life is an age-old pursuit that weaves through the fabric of human existence. It speaks to the very core of who we are, the choices we make, and the paths we follow. The search for meaning often begins in moments of reflection, where we pause and consider not just the what of our lives but the why. Why do we rise each morning? What fuels our passions? What do we care about deeply enough to fight for? These questions form the foundation of our purpose, propelling us forward even in the face of adversity.

Philosophers and psychologists alike have emphasised the importance of purpose. Viktor Frankl, a Holocaust survivor and psychiatrist, encapsulated this in his seminal work, "Man's Search for Meaning." He argued that the pursuit of meaning, rather than pleasure or power, is the primary motivational force in human beings. For Frankl, those who find a profound sense of purpose can endure unimaginable hardships. His insights remind us that our reasons for living can sustain us through tough times, validating the belief that purpose is not a luxury but a necessity.

Purpose provides direction. It acts as a compass, guiding us through life's complexities. When we understand our "why," decision-making becomes clearer. As we navigate various paths, knowing our purpose helps filter the noise from the signal. Every choice we make, from career paths to relationships, can align more closely with our core values when we are anchored in our purpose.

The Power of Becoming

This alignment creates a sense of coherence in our lives, allowing us to connect the dots between our experiences and aspirations.

To delve deeper into the significance of purpose, it is important to explore the interlinking of interests, values, and broader life goals. Start by identifying what truly ignites your spirit. Reflect on moments in your life when you felt completely engaged, alive, and excited. What were you doing? Who were you with? These experiences often serve as windows into our core interests. They are the building blocks from which we can start to construct a sense of purpose.

As you pinpoint these interests, the next step is to investigate how they align with your values. Values are the beliefs that shape our attitudes and behaviours, often serving as guiding principles in our lives. They encompass what we deem important and serve as a moral framework. Consider what values resonate with you on a personal level. Is it honesty? Creativity? Compassion? Empowerment? Each value you identify not only reflects your beliefs but also shapes your motivations, informing your sense of purpose.

To engage more deeply with these reflective exercises, take some time to journal about your interests and values. Write freely without concern for structure. Begin with your interests and note down every activity or subject that captivates you. Ask yourself questions like: When do I lose track of time? What topics do I eagerly discuss or read about? What hobbies do I feel most passionate about? Allow your mind to wander and write whatever comes to heart.

The Power of Becoming

Next, take a moment to list your values. What traits do you admire in others? What principles guide your actions? Write down the top five values that resonate most with you. Once you have your lists, draw connections between the two. How can your interests serve as a vehicle for your values? If one of your interests is writing but your value is empathy, perhaps you can write stories that convey the importance of understanding different perspectives. This exercise is not merely an act of self-exploration; it is a direct bridge to uncovering your "why."

This connection serves as an impetus to identify specific life goals. By connecting your interests and values, you might discover that your purpose points toward a particular direction, such as advocating for social justice, fostering creativity in education, or empowering others through mentorship. As you reflect on these connections, consider the impact you want to leave on the world. What legacy do you wish to create?

Often, defining our legacy can clarify our purpose. Consider the broader context of your community, your world, and even future generations. How can your interests and values collide to create a meaningful impact? This inward-looking exercise allows for an outward exploration of purpose, forging a connection between your individual aspirations and the collective well-being of society.

Engaging with these reflective exercises also primes you for deeper introspection. Vulnerability often accompanies this journey. It is natural to encounter discomfort when examining your true motivations. Yet embracing this discomfort can be transformative. This process invites you to face your fears and doubts, empowering you to redefine failure and persist in your pursuit of purpose.

The Power of Becoming

Throughout history, countless individuals have harnessed their purpose to create iconic narratives of personal and collective growth. Consider figures like Nelson Mandela, whose purpose drove him to dismantle apartheid in South Africa, despite enduring 27 years in prison. His commitment to fighting for justice and equality not only defined his legacy but also inspired countless others to stand up for their beliefs.

Yet one's purpose doesn't need to have global implications. Purpose is inherently personal and can manifest in many different forms. You may find your purpose in the small, everyday actions that contribute to the happiness and well-being of those around you. This could range from nurturing your family and being a supportive friend to fostering creativity in your workplace or volunteering in your community. Regardless of how grand or modest your purpose may appear, what matters is the authenticity of your journey toward discovering it.

Recognise that purpose is not a static destination but a fluid journey that evolves with your life experiences, interests, and desires. In a world teeming with distractions and noise, taking time to reflect on your purpose can be both grounding and liberating. It encourages living with intention rather than drifting through life at the mercy of external forces.

Consider implementing regular purpose check-ins where you revisit the insights uncovered during your reflective exercises. Ask yourself whether your current path aligns with your interests and values. Are your daily actions and choices bringing you closer to understanding your "why"? Cultivating a purpose-driven mindset can elevate your motivation and infuse your life with fulfilment.

When dropouts become high school leaders who refuse to settle for mediocrity, and hospital orderlies lift spirits through compassion rather than just care, they showcase the compelling impact purpose can have on our perceptions of ourselves and the world.

Finally, share your journey with others. By vocalising your "why," you not only reinforce your commitments but also invite accountability. Discussing your purpose with friends, family, mentors, or a support group can create opportunities for encouragement, feedback, and growth. This communal aspect of purpose not only enhances individual journeys but can also foster shared missions that uplift entire communities.

In conclusion, discovering your purpose, a journey into your heart and mind, challenges you to engage with the world around you more meaningfully. It encourages you to connect with your passions, align your actions with your values, and move toward impactful contributions. With an understanding that exploring purpose is a lifelong endeavour, embrace the process of becoming. Each step taken toward discovering your "why" is a powerful move toward becoming your best self. By allowing the insights of your narrative to shape your purpose, you create a roadmap not just for survival but for a life rich with meaning, fulfilment, and profound connection.

Aligning Passions and Values

Aligning your passions and values is a pivotal step in becoming your best self. Many of us navigate life with a vague sense of what we love and what we believe in, but aligning these two crucial elements is key to discovering your true "why." Passion ignites energy and enthusiasm, while values provide direction and purpose. When you

The Power of Becoming

successfully harmonise both, you create a powerful anchor that guides you through life's ups and downs.

To embark on this journey of alignment, it is essential to first understand what true passion and core values mean to each individual. Passion is that intense, driving force that compels you to pursue what you adore. It can manifest in various forms, such as hobbies, careers, social causes, or even daily activities. Values, on the other hand, are your personal beliefs about what is important in life. They reflect your morals, ethics, and priorities, guiding your decisions and interactions.

The intersection of passions and values creates a potent synergy. When you engage in activities that resonate with your values, you are not only happier but also more productive and fulfilled. Conversely, pursuing passions that do not align with your core values can lead to feelings of disconnection, frustration, and even burnout. Thus, gaining clarity on both fronts is essential to living a life of meaning.

Compiling a list of your passions can be an enlightening exercise. Begin by exploring various aspects of your life: What activities do you lose track of time while doing? What subjects ignite a fire within you? Reflect on moments that have brought you immense joy or satisfaction. Write down the activities that come to mind, even if they seem trivial at first, because they could serve as integral pieces of your authentic self.

Next, shift your focus to your core values. Consider what principles govern your decision-making. Use prompts such as "What do you stand for?" When do you feel most fulfilled? What do you want to be remembered for? Delve into both personal and professional contexts. Honesty, integrity, empathy, adventure, creativity: these are just a few examples. Again, jot it all down.

Once you have a comprehensive list of your passions and values, the real work begins: identifying the connections between the two. Draw a map of your passions on one side and your values on the other. Look for overlaps or intersections. How do your passions reflect your values? How do your values inform your passions? This visual representation can provide insight into areas where you find alignment and can also illuminate elements of your life that may feel disjointed.

Next, engage in practical exercises to deepen your understanding of this alignment.

One exercise is the "Passion Inventory." For one week, capture your daily activities in a notebook. Rate each activity on a scale of 1 to 10 based on how much joy it brings you, how engaging it is, and whether it aligns with your core values. At the end of the week, review your entries for patterns. Which activities are frequently rated highly? Which did not? This will help you identify passions that resonate most deeply with you and the changes you might need to make to live in greater alignment with your values.

Another effective exercise is "Value Validation." Choose a few of your core values and reflect on how well they are represented in your daily life. Ask yourself questions such as: Am I living in accordance with my value of integrity? Do my daily choices reflect my commitment to creativity? Are there friendships or commitments that do not align with my values? This reflective process may lead to meaningful shifts in your relationships or daily routines.

The Power of Becoming

A helpful tool in this exploration is vision mapping. This technique allows you to envision your ideal life as it relates to both your passions and values. Find a quiet place, take a deep breath, and visualise your future. Picture a day in your life where your passions and values are perfectly aligned. What are you doing? Who are you with? How do you feel? Write down this vision in detail. Once you have created your vision, break it down into achievable goals. What steps do you need to take to get closer to this vision? These small goals will provide the momentum you need to move forward. Keep this vision map visible to remind you of your "why" on days when inspiration wanes.

Real-life stories can serve as powerful motivators throughout this process. Take, for example, the story of Mia, a corporate professional who felt a growing discontent with her career. Although she was successful by societal standards, she realised that her job did not resonate with her core value of community service. After participating in workshops focused on self-discovery, Mia began volunteering in her local community, aligning her passion for helping others with her value of service. This newfound clarity led her to inspire her company to implement community service days, enabling her colleagues to connect their work with their own passions. Mia's journey illustrates that aligning your passions with your values can lead to broader impacts, personally and professionally.

Similarly, consider the narrative of James, who spent years in academia chasing accolades in a field that did not ignite his passion. It was not until he took the time to identify his core values: creativity, freedom, and connection, that he realised he was meant to be an artist. He began investing his time in creative projects, leading him to teach art classes that fulfilled his purpose, not just for

The Power of Becoming

him but for his students as well. James' decision to transition into a creative career allowed him to influence others, thereby amplifying the richness of his own life.

As you reflect on these examples, think about how realignment can create ripple effects beyond your individual self. When you align your passions and values, you not only enrich your own life but also inspire those around you. Conversations will deepen, relationships will enrich, and your influence will expand.

The significance of aligning passions and values extends beyond personal fulfilment; it nourishes the fundamental human desire for connection. When you are clear on what you stand for and what drives you, you become more authentic in your relationships. This authenticity invites vulnerability and deepens connections with others who understand you and resonate with the values that shape your life.

As you refine your alignment, remember to stay flexible. Life is dynamic, and as you grow, your passions and values may shift. Regular check-ins on your lists and vision map can help you remain in tune with yourself. Set aside time, perhaps biannually or annually, to reassess your passions and values. Are they still reflective of who you are? If not, take the time to recalibrate your compass.

Finally, as you embrace this journey of alignment, be patient with yourself. Discovering your true "why" and aligning your passions with your values is not a destination; it is an ongoing process. Celebrate the small wins, learn from setbacks, and observe how your journey evolves. Each step taken toward alignment is a testament to your commitment to becoming your best self.

The Power of Becoming

In the end, the power of becoming resides in your ability to connect: the connections within yourself as you blend your passions and values, and the connections you foster with others as you share your journey. Aligning passions and values is not just about you; it extends to the collective tapestry of lives you touch along the way. Embrace your journey, honour your authentic self, and recognise the profound impact of living a life rooted in purpose. As you align your passions with your values, you are not merely existing; you are truly becoming.

Drafting Your Mission Statement

The concept of a mission statement may seem abstract or even overly formal, but crafting your personal mission statement is a pivotal exercise that can anchor you powerfully in your journey of becoming your best self. A mission statement provides clarity to your purpose, guiding your actions, decisions, and priorities. As you delve into the process of defining your "why," this subchapter offers a structured framework that will help you articulate your unique mission in life.

Understanding the Importance of a Personal Mission Statement

Before diving into the drafting process, it is crucial to understand why a mission statement matters. It serves as your North Star, a guiding principle that shapes your behaviour and thoughts. It keeps you centred, especially during challenging times, and helps ensure your goals align with your true values and passions. With this clarity, decision-making becomes simpler. You learn to say OK to what aligns with your mission and no to what detracts from it.

Consider how a clearly articulated mission statement can influence various facets of your life, from career choices to interpersonal relationships. It is not merely a statement to be read and forgotten but a living document that evolves as you grow. It encapsulates your values, passions, and goals, serving as a reminder of what truly matters to you.

The Structured Framework for Crafting Your Mission Statement

To draft a meaningful personal mission statement, you can follow a structured framework consisting of four stages: Reflect, Define, Write, and Refine. Each of these stages is essential in shaping a comprehensive, authentic, and powerful mission statement.

Reflect

The first step in crafting your mission statement is reflection. This is a deep dive into your thoughts, feelings, and experiences to uncover what resonates with you. Consider these reflective prompts:

1. What are my core values?
2. Identifying your values is fundamental. What principles govern your life and decisions? Values such as honesty, compassion, creativity, and courage can form the cornerstone of your mission.
3. What are my passions?
4. What activities or topics ignite a fire in you? Reflect on moments when you felt most alive and fulfilled.
5. What are my unique gifts?

6. Everyone possesses unique talents that can contribute to the world. Reflect on skills or strengths that set you apart.
7. What legacy do I want to leave?
8. Imagine looking back on your life. What contributions do you wish to be remembered for?
9. What have been my past experiences?
10. Reflect on significant events, positive and negative, that have shaped you.

Make time for this phase through journaling, meditation, or quiet contemplation. Allow yourself the space to explore your thoughts fully.

Define

Once you have completed your reflection, the next step is to define what you have uncovered. Distil your insights into themes and elements for your mission statement.

1. Identify Key Themes
2. Look for patterns or recurring ideas in your reflections.
3. Set Your Direction
4. Consider what behaviours and actions will embody your mission.
5. Craft the Core Elements
6. A strong statement includes your purpose, the audience you wish to serve, and an expression of your unique approach.
7. Connect Goals to Your Why
8. Ensure your goals align with your values and purpose.

Write

The Power of Becoming

With your reflections and definitions ready, begin crafting the statement itself.

1. Be Concise but Comprehensive
2. A few sentences can often be more impactful than a long paragraph.
3. Use Positive Language
4. Focus on what you want to create.
5. Make it Inspiring
6. Use language that motivates you.
7. Envision the Audience
8. Consider who your mission seeks to serve.
9. Write Different Drafts
10. Experiment freely until you find the right fit.
11. Read Aloud
12. This helps to identify awkward phrasing.

Refine

Once you have a draft:

1. Seek Feedback
2. Trusted friends, family, or mentors can offer valuable insight.
3. Revisit Your Themes
4. Ensure the statement reflects your core values and passions.
5. Embrace Evolution
6. Your mission may evolve.
7. Make it Visible
8. Place it somewhere you will see it daily.
9. Live it Out

10. Begin implementing behaviours aligned with your mission.

Conclusion: The Ongoing Journey of Refinement

Drafting your mission statement is an enriching process that lays the groundwork for profound personal growth. It is not the end but the beginning. Embrace your mission as a living document that you revisit and refine throughout your life.

In conclusion, drafting your mission statement is an invaluable exercise that connects you to your "why." It provides clarity and direction as you embark on your unique journey. By reflecting on your values, defining your themes, writing a compelling statement, and refining it over time, you create a powerful testament to your purpose and aspirations.

Now is the perfect time to take the next step. Embrace this opportunity to articulate your mission and let it illuminate the path toward your best self.

Contribution and Impact

The Ripple Effect of Contribution

The concept of the ripple effect is a powerful metaphor that illustrates how a single action can create a chain reaction of positive consequences. Just as a pebble thrown into a still pond sends out ripples across the water, one person's contribution can extend far beyond their immediate surroundings, impacting lives, communities and even societies in ways that might not be immediately evident. This subchapter explores the profound nature of these ripples, demonstrating how our choices, actions and contributions can lead to meaningful change in the world around us.

To understand the ripple effect, we must first acknowledge the inherent interconnectedness of our lives. Every interaction we have, every decision we make, reverberates through the fabric of our communities. These ripples can inspire, motivate and uplift others, creating a collective momentum that becomes a force for positive change. When we engage in acts of contribution, whether volunteering time, sharing knowledge or offering emotional support, we set off a series of reactions that can lead to transformations on both personal and societal levels.

Consider the story of a young woman named Maya, who discovered the dire need for mental health support in her high school. Growing up, she faced challenges related to anxiety and depression, but struggled to find the resources and support she needed. After overcoming her own obstacles, she felt compelled to help others who faced similar struggles.

The Power of Becoming

Maya decided to initiate a weekly peer support group, where students could come together to share their experiences and offer one another encouragement. Initially, she started with a handful of students who were also grappling with their mental health. The group provided a safe space for vulnerability, understanding and connection. As word spread, more students began attending, and the group's impact grew.

Not only did participants feel less isolated, but they also took their newfound insights back to their classrooms, fostering a culture of empathy and support that transformed the school environment. Teachers noticed a reduction in absenteeism and an increase in students' overall well-being among those who participated. Maya's contribution did not end at her school; it inspired schools in the surrounding area to establish similar programmes, creating a network of support that extended beyond geographical boundaries. Her initial action triggered a wave of change, showcasing how one person's contribution can create ripples of transformation that touch the lives of many.

Every ripple has the potential to touch multiple lives, each of which can in turn create its own ripples. Take, for instance, the story of James, a retiree passionate about literacy. After a fulfilling career as a teacher, he noticed that many adults in his community struggled with reading and writing. He volunteered at a local community centre, teaching basic literacy skills to adults on Saturdays.

Although he started with a few individuals, word of mouth soon led to larger classes. The impact was not limited to the adult learners; as they gained literacy skills, their confidence grew, and they became more engaged in their families and communities. Many went on to help their children with homework and navigate everyday tasks such as understanding bills or applying for jobs. James had set off a ripple effect of increased literacy, breaking cycles of disadvantage in families, empowering one person to broaden another's world and opportunities.

These stories underline an essential truth: contributions can inspire a collective awakening and a readiness to embrace change within communities. The ripple effect, however, requires intentionality and awareness. It emphasises that our actions, however small, are significant. As we contribute to others, we elevate ourselves and those around us. This collective elevation can lead to a culture of giving, where acts of kindness, mentorship and support become normalised.

A powerful example of this culture taking root can be witnessed in the initiative called "Pay It Forward," which encourages individuals to carry out acts of kindness for others. One instance highlighted a man named David, who decided to pay for the coffee of the person behind him in line at his local café. This simple act sparked a chain reaction, where countless subsequent customers chose to do the same.

This movement showcased how small gestures can inspire others to contribute in their own ways. The initial act of kindness became a catalyst for broader community engagement, prompting individuals to seek out opportunities to help others. The effect of such actions goes beyond the immediate act; it cultivates an environment where kindness flourishes. Each person involved is reminded of their ability to make a difference, no matter how small.

By contributing to our communities, we also challenge prevailing narratives that emphasise isolation and individualism in modern society. When we adopt a mind-set rooted in contribution, we acknowledge our role in the interconnected web of humanity. The impact of this shift can be seen in a multitude of social movements addressing issues such as climate change, social justice and poverty. Each of these movements is fuelled by individual contributions and shared passions, collectively aiming to create significant change.

A poignant example is the global environmental movement driven by activists like Greta Thunberg. Starting with her solitary school strike for climate action, Greta's determination to address climate change has inspired millions of young people worldwide to join advocacy efforts. Her story is a testament to the ripple effect; one individual's commitment to a cause can mobilise an entire generation and spur widespread action across borders.

As individuals rally for change, they not only contribute to a larger cause but also become empowered to take on leadership and influence roles. This phenomenon highlights another dimension of the ripple effect: empowerment. When we contribute to something larger than ourselves, we are often transformed in the process. We develop new skills, enhance our empathy and expand our perspectives.

Looking outward, the act of contributing can awaken a sense of purpose within us, propelling us to seek further contributions. This may manifest as a commitment to volunteerism, advocacy or community building. Each contribution feeds the desire for service, creating a loop of encouragement that invites more individuals into the fold.

The Power of Becoming

Embracing the ripple effect requires a mind-set shift. Instead of seeing our contributions as isolated events, we must envision them as part of a larger tapestry of interconnected actions. Not every contribution will create an immediate or visible impact, but that does not diminish its significance. We may not always witness the ripples our actions create, yet they still ripple through lives and communities, shaping a brighter future.

As we think about our potential contributions, it is vital to explore our unique skills and passions. Where can you make a difference? What issues resonate with your values? Perhaps you love to cook. Sharing meals with those in need could spark a nourishing movement in your neighbourhood. If you are an artist, your creative expression might inspire conversations or healing in a community grappling with pain.

In finding our individual contributions, we practise tuning into the needs around us. Listening, observing and engaging can illuminate avenues for meaningful impact. Whether you choose to mentor a young person, organise community clean-ups, or support local businesses, each action has the potential to reverberate.

Moreover, we should remain open to collaboration. Often, the ripples that lead to significant change occur when individual contributions converge. Collaborative efforts amplify our impact, attracting diverse perspectives and resources. For example, local non-profits may work together towards a common goal, each bringing their unique skills and networks to the table.

We can also cultivate a culture of contribution, encouraging others to join us in making a difference. Storytelling plays a pivotal role here; sharing our experiences, whether small or significant, can

The Power of Becoming

motivate others to act. Speaking about our contributions and their impacts openly serves dual purposes: it honours the journey of contribution while inspiring others to embark on their own paths. Communities thrive on collective narratives, and by sharing these stories, we keep the momentum of change alive.

Yet we must approach our contributions with humility. The impact of our actions may not always align with our intentions. This is where reflection becomes vital. Regularly assessing our contributions helps us learn how to engage more effectively with others. Recognising that the ripple effect can sometimes yield unintended consequences helps us navigate our roles as contributors with consciousness and adaptability.

As we take steps to become our best selves, we must embrace the responsibility carried within our contributions. Each time we act with intention, we reaffirm our commitment to the interconnectedness of humanity. This requires us to cultivate not only individual contributions but a community that values and celebrates collective impact.

In conclusion, the ripple effect of contributions is a profound testament to the potential each of us holds to shape a better world. By recognising the power of our actions, we can ignite change not only in our own lives but also in those around us. Let Maya's journey inspire you to start a conversation in your school, community or workplace. Join James in promoting literacy and education, and enlist the help of friends and colleagues to multiply your impact.

Consider how your small act could transform lives. Find your way to contribute, however discreetly, and observe how each ripple can create waves of change. You hold the power to influence, uplift and inspire. Embrace that power and watch as your contributions create ripples of transformation that extend far beyond your immediate reach. Today is the day to start your own ripple; tomorrow, you might witness the waves of change it inspires.

Make your contribution count, and who knows how many lives may be touched in the process. The journey of becoming is not just about personal growth; it is about recognising and harnessing our collective potential to impact the world around us.

Eliciting a Call to Service

Service, in its myriad forms, serves as a remarkable conduit for personal growth and self-discovery. Within each of us lies an innate desire to make a difference, to contribute to the world around us. As we begin to explore the profound impact of service on our lives, we discover not only the power of giving but also the transformative journey it prompts within ourselves. Engaging in community service enriches our lives by deepening connections, enhancing our understanding of diverse perspectives and nurturing a sense of purpose that resonates well beyond the act of giving.

The process of eliciting a call to service can unfold in numerous ways. It often begins with introspection, examining our values, passions and the issues that ignite a fire within us. This exploration helps us recognise the causes that resonate personally, transforming abstract notions of service into concrete actions. As we align our efforts with our core beliefs, we embark on a path that is not only fulfilling but also authentic.

The Power of Becoming

To fully grasp the essence of service as a means of personal growth, let us first consider how giving to others fosters a deeper understanding of ourselves. When we engage in acts of service, we open ourselves to new experiences and perspectives that challenge us to step outside our comfort zones. We learn empathy, resilience, teamwork and compassion, all qualities that enrich our character and contribute to our personal development.

Moreover, service taps into our ability to connect. Human beings are inherently social creatures. By serving others, we forge bonds with diverse individuals from various walks of life. These connections can provide us with fresh insights and broaden our horizons, ultimately transforming how we view the world around us. Each interaction has the potential to teach us more about ourselves, enhancing our self-awareness and leading us to reflect on our roles within our communities.

With this understanding, the next step is to turn reflection into action. Here are practical steps to help readers get involved in community service and contribute actively to the causes they are passionate about:

1. **Identify Your Passion:**

Take time to reflect on the causes that resonate deeply with you. It could be environmental conservation, education, health care, poverty alleviation, animal welfare or social justice. Creating a list of potential causes can help you see where your interest lies.

2. **Research Opportunities:**

The Power of Becoming

Once you have a clear sense of your passions, research organisations and initiatives that align with those interests. Check local charities, non-profit organisations and community service programmes. VolunteerMatch and Idealist are excellent platforms to discover opportunities that suit your skills and availability.

3. Start Small:

If committing time feels overwhelming, start small. Even a few hours a month can make a significant impact. You can lend a hand at a local food bank, participate in community clean-up days or help organise events for charitable causes. Starting small allows you to integrate service into your life without feeling burdened.

4. Engage with Others:

Do not underestimate the power of collaboration. Engaging with friends or family members can enhance your volunteer experience and motivate you to stay committed. It adds a layer of accountability and enjoyment, turning service into a shared journey. Forming a service group with like-minded individuals can amplify your impact and strengthen connections.

5. Embrace Learning:

As you engage in service, remain open to learning from every experience. Each act of giving provides insights into the struggles and triumphs of those around you. Listen to stories, ask questions and reflect on how your efforts contribute to change. Being a learner allows you to adapt your approaches and stay engaged in the cause.

6. Reflect and Evaluate:

After participating in a service activity or volunteering, take time to reflect on your experience. What did you learn? How did it make you feel? What impact do you believe you had? This evaluation deepens your understanding of service and can influence how you continue to engage with the community.

7. Share Your Journey:

Documenting and sharing your service experiences can inspire others to join in the effort. Whether through social media, blogs or community gatherings, sharing your story creates a ripple effect that can encourage others to explore their own call to service. This collective sharing enhances community engagement and fosters a culture of giving.

8. Stay Committed:

The path of service is not a sprint; it is a marathon. Commit to continuous learning and engagement with the causes you care about. As you grow, your understanding of issues may deepen, leading to new avenues for contribution. Embrace the long-term journey.

9. Cultivate Gratitude:

The Power of Becoming

In serving others, we often find appreciation for our own circumstances. Cultivating gratitude for what we have while helping those who may have less sharpens our perspective and fosters a more profound sense of connection to humanity. Regular gratitude practices can enhance your overall well-being and motivate you along your service journey.

While these practical steps provide a framework for getting involved, it is essential to acknowledge the deeper significance of service. Serving others often requires vulnerability: acknowledging our limitations and being open to the experiences of those we seek to help. In stepping away from our own needs and desires, we come to understand what it means to put others first. This selflessness creates opportunities for immense personal growth and often leads to feelings of fulfilment we may not have anticipated.

Consider the stories of individuals who have answered their own calls to service. Each has faced moments of doubt, confusion, and uncertainty, yet those who persevere often find their lives transformed in ways they could never have foreseen. A woman who began volunteering at a local shelter found her calling in social work and ultimately dedicated her life to helping those in marginalised communities. A young man who started a small initiative focused on educational outreach saw it blossom into a non-profit organisation that now serves thousands of underprivileged children.

These narratives highlight a powerful truth: as we extend ourselves in service, we invite profound personal transformation. It is in giving that our own identities can evolve, revealing aspects of ourselves we may never have discovered if we remained solely inward-focused. Each encounter with those we aim to serve can teach us resilience, empathy and adaptability, qualities essential for navigating life's challenges.

Furthermore, the relationships we build through service can serve as a stronghold during tumultuous times. The connections made may offer support when we face our struggles. Community service can forge friendships that provide comfort, encouragement and understanding, enriching our lives beyond the act itself.

It is vital to remember that the impact of service extends beyond mere outcomes; it transforms both the giver and the receiver. When we choose to lend a helping hand, we become active participants in shaping the world around us. Our efforts contribute to a larger narrative of compassion, solidarity and transformation. In this way, our personal growth creates ripple effects that positively influence our communities and ultimately the world.

In conclusion, eliciting a call to service is about creating a tangible connection between our inner motivations and their outward expressions in the world. It emphasises that our journey of becoming our best selves does not happen in isolation. Instead, it flourishes in the company of others, particularly those whom we uplift through our service. As we heed this call, we not only foster our own development but also become agents of change, actively participating in the collective journey towards a brighter future.

Embrace this call to service not just as a duty but as a pathway to unlocking your greatest potential. Allow it to deepen your understanding and compassion, and witness the transformation it brings not only to your life but to the lives of those you touch. The journey of becoming continues beyond individual achievement and finds its richest expression through giving, growing and connecting with others. Take that step today, serve and begin unravelling the beautiful tapestry of personal growth that bursts forth through service.

Legacy: The Long-Term Impacts

Legacy is often viewed through the lens of permanence; it is about what remains after we are gone and how our lives and actions resonate through time. Focusing on the long-term effects of personal contributions, this subchapter invites readers to consider the legacies they wish to leave behind, encouraging profound reflection on their values, actions and the mark they wish to leave on the world.

To begin, we must contemplate the notion of legacy itself. What do we wish people to remember about us? What stories will our grandchildren tell about us? The way we live our lives today ripples outwards, impacting our communities, loved ones and beyond, forming narratives that can inspire and uplift others long after we are gone. Whether these legacies are positive or negative often hinges on our choices and contributions throughout our lifetimes.

Take, for instance, the legacy of a teacher who dedicates decades to instilling in her students a love for learning and a sense of possibility. Ms Wilson, a passionate educator in a struggling neighbourhood, pours her heart into her work. She stays late at school to help struggling students with their homework and creates an after-school programme that engages children in productive and creative activities.

Her impact may not be quantifiable in the moment; standardised test scores may provide a limited view of her contribution. But over the years, her students graduate, go on to pursue higher education, and some even return to the community to give back. The legacy she leaves is not merely one of academic success; it is rooted in empowerment, belief in potential and the nurturing of resilient individuals who, in turn, shape their own legacies.

Similarly, consider the story of a family that comes together to support a local charity. Every Thanksgiving, the Garcia family volunteers at a homeless shelter, serving meals and connecting with those in need. For them, the act of giving back has become a cherished tradition, one that they pass down to their children.

Each year, as the children grow, they assume more responsibility, helping to cook, engaging with guests, and even raising funds for the shelter. As adults, these children carry the values learned from their parents into their own families, continuing the cycle of service and compassion. The Garcias are not simply creating a seasonal habit; they are establishing a legacy of kindness, community involvement and social responsibility that will endure well beyond their years, encouraging future generations to act with empathy and purpose.

In both narratives, the legacies form a continuous thread, weaving through time and connecting lives in meaningful ways. Such legacies may stem from countless sources, from a commitment to family or community service to artistic ventures or innovations in various fields. The commonality among all successful legacies is a commitment to selflessness; they thrive on the intention to uplift others, create opportunities and contribute to a greater good.

However, it is essential to recognise that grand, dramatic actions do not define legacy in isolation. Often, the most impactful legacies are born from consistent, small acts of kindness and mindfulness in our daily lives.

Consider someone like Mr Thompson, a neighbour in a quiet community. He takes the time each week to mow the lawns of elderly residents who are no longer able to do so themselves. He listens to their stories, shares a laugh and offers companionship. His actions may seem minor in the grand scheme of life, but the sense of community he fosters leaves a lasting impression on his neighbours.

The legacy he creates is built on connection, care and friendship, a legacy rooted in the simple understanding that everyone deserves dignity and love.

These illustrations highlight how legacies are shaped not just through grand gestures but through the deep, purposeful connections we create with others. They remind us that we all have the potential to leave behind a positive impact, regardless of our circumstances. As we consider our own legacies, it is vital to reflect on how we interact with those around us and how we respond to challenges in our lives.

Another vital component of legacy is the values we choose to embody. Values are the compass guiding our actions and decisions, shaping not only our lives but also the lives of those who witness our choices. A strong commitment to justice, for instance, can inspire others to stand up for what is right in their own spheres of influence. An individual who advocates for environmental sustainability may encourage family, friends and subsequent generations to embrace the importance of caring for the planet. In this way, our legacies become intertwined with broader cultural narratives, shaping societal values and priorities over time.

Moreover, legacies can also stem from adversity and resilience. Take the case of someone who has faced significant personal challenges; their journey of overcoming obstacles can serve as a powerful testament to perseverance.

Let us examine the story of Alice, who grew up in a tumultuous home, battling against neglect and adversity. Instead of allowing her experiences to define her negatively, she channels her struggles into motivation, pursuing higher education and nurturing a deep desire to support at-risk youth. Her work in mentorship and advocacy not only empowers the young people she serves but also illustrates how obstacles can breed resilience and inspire others to see that no circumstance is too great to overcome.

Alice's story resonates beyond her immediate impact, encouraging individuals to face their struggles head-on and inspire those around them to do the same.

In addition, consider individuals whose lives are shaped by their craft or artistic endeavours. Artists, musicians and writers often leave legacies that transcend their lifetimes through their work. The rich tapestry of cultural history is interwoven with the legacies of figures like Maya Angelou, Frida Kahlo and Beethoven. Each of these individuals contributed profoundly to their respective fields, sparking thought, emotion and change. Their legacies continue to inspire, provoke and challenge generations to come, reminding us of the power of expression and the importance of authenticity in our work.

The Power of Becoming

As we delve deeper into the idea of legacy, it is crucial to recognise the potential of collective contributions. When communities come together to effect change, the impact can be monumental. Movements founded on shared values and visions for a better future demonstrate the incredible influence of united action.

An example can be found in the civil rights movement. Leaders like Martin Luther King Jr., Rosa Parks, and countless others galvanised individuals from diverse backgrounds to fight for equality and justice. Their collective efforts led to transformative changes in society, establishing a legacy that continues to inspire global movements for rights and freedoms today.

In conceiving our own legacies, we must ponder where we fit into the fabric of our communities and the world at large. Understanding the importance of collaborative efforts can encourage us to forge connections with others, recognising that our individual contributions are often magnified when aligned with a shared goal. A sense of interconnectedness fosters support and camaraderie, reinforcing the idea that together we can create lasting change.

As we envision our legacy, it can be helpful to adopt a long-term perspective. This requires us to step outside our immediate concerns and see the broader picture of how our actions affect future generations. We need to ask ourselves tough questions: What issues do we care about deeply? How can we become advocates for change? What narratives do we hope to pass down to our children and grandchildren? By creating this framework, we can better navigate our choices and contributions with a sense of purpose.

The Power of Becoming

To solidify our legacy, we can embody our values and pursue passionate causes throughout our lives. Engaging in volunteer work, championing advocacy or simply committing to kindness in our daily interactions can serve as stepping stones toward leaving a lasting impact. Reflective practices, such as maintaining a journal, can help us understand our motivations and solidify our ambitions, clarifying the legacy we wish to leave behind.

Moreover, legacy is ever-evolving. It constantly adapts in response to our actions and decisions. It is essential to remain open to feedback and be willing to adjust our approaches. Legacy is not only about what we have done but also about how we grow and learn. As we navigate life's complexities, we must accept that our journey will be an assemblage of successes and failures, all of which contribute to our understanding of our desires and the essence of our legacies.

In conclusion, contemplating our legacies is an invitation to shape our lives with intention. It allows us to reflect on how we wish to be remembered, ensuring our contributions resonate long into the future. By embracing selflessness, connection, shared values and resilience, we can craft legacies that inspire future generations to embrace their power to create change.

The stories we share, the love we give and the challenges we overcome all blend to create an impact that extends well beyond our own existence. Thus, as we journey through life, let us commit to becoming aware of the legacy we are building, one choice at a time.

Becoming Never Ends

Embracing Continuous Learning

Lifelong learning is a concept that transcends age, profession and personal circumstance. It embodies the idea that the journey of growth and self-discovery never truly ends; rather, it is a continuous cycle of exploration, adaptation and enrichment. In a rapidly changing world, the ability to learn continuously is not just advantageous; it is essential.

This subchapter delves into the power of continuous learning as a pivotal element of personal evolution, exploring how curiosity and a steadfast commitment to growth cultivate resilience and empower individuals to reach their fullest potential.

At the heart of lifelong learning lies an innate curiosity, the desire to explore, question and understand. Curious exploration often begins in childhood, where every question is an opportunity for discovery. However, as we transition into adulthood, societal norms and expectations may stifle this natural inquisitiveness. We can fall into the trap of complacency, believing that we are either too busy or too settled in our ways to pursue new knowledge.

This is where the commitment to continuous learning becomes both a challenge and an opportunity. By consciously choosing to embrace a mind-set of curiosity, we can break free from the confines of routine and open ourselves to new experiences, ideas, and perspectives.

The Power of Becoming

The world today demands adaptability. As technological advancements and societal shifts occur at an unprecedented pace, those unwilling to learn and grow risk obsolescence. New innovations are transforming every industry, and skills that were once in high demand can become outdated in a matter of years. This reality underscores the importance of cultivating a lifelong learning mind-set. Those who actively pursue knowledge and development are better equipped to navigate an ever-evolving landscape.

Continuous learning is not just about acquiring new skills; it also fosters resilience. When we engage in the process of learning, we are inevitably faced with challenges, mistakes and setbacks. These moments are not just obstacles; they are growth opportunities. Each time we confront a difficulty, whether in mastering a complex concept, completing a challenging course or attempting a new skill, we practise perseverance and develop a growth mind-set.

We learn to view challenges not as insurmountable barriers but as integral steps in our journey. This resilience nurtured through learning becomes a powerful asset that enables us to face adversity with confidence and adaptability.

One practical approach to embracing continuous learning is to incorporate learning into our daily lives. This can take many forms, from reading widely to participating in structured courses. The key is to find what resonates with you and make a conscious effort to integrate it into your routine.

Reading, for instance, is one of the simplest yet most effective ways to fuel your lifelong learning journey. By selecting books that challenge your thinking or expand your knowledge in areas of interest, you can transform your daily commute, lunch breaks or

The Power of Becoming

evenings into valuable learning experiences. Whether it is fiction that opens your imagination, biographies that inspire you or non-fiction that informs your professional growth, each page offers an opportunity to expand your horizons.

Online courses and workshops have also emerged as invaluable resources for those seeking to learn. Platforms offering a wide range of subjects, from coding and design to personal development and leadership, empower individuals to learn at their own pace. The flexibility of online learning allows you to customise your educational pathway, ensuring it aligns with your personal interests and professional goals. Allocating a few hours each week to a course you are passionate about can catalyse significant transformation, allowing you to acquire skills that can enhance your career or deepen your understanding of specific topics.

Moreover, learning is not confined to formal education or solitary pursuits. Engaging in experiences can yield profound insights and lessons that enhance our personal growth. Look for opportunities to learn through travel, volunteering or community involvement. By immersing yourself in different cultures, meeting diverse individuals and embracing new challenges, you expand your worldview and develop a range of skills that transcend traditional learning environments. These experiences encourage adaptability, empathy and a deeper appreciation for the complexities of the human experience.

Networking is another powerful avenue for continuous learning. Surrounding yourself with diverse groups of people, those who share your interests as well as those who challenge your viewpoints, can facilitate rich discussions and spur your intellectual growth. Join professional organisations, attend conferences or participate in local meet-ups focused on your areas of interest. These interactions not only provide valuable insights but also encourage the exchange of new ideas and practices.

Reflecting on what you have learned is just as critical as the act of learning itself. Keeping a learning journal or engaging in self-reflection helps reinforce your understanding and retain knowledge more effectively. After completing a book or course, take time to synthesise what you have learned. Ask yourself how you can apply these concepts in your life. What resonated with you? What challenged your previous beliefs? By integrating reflection into your learning process, you reinforce the lessons and deepen your understanding, making the knowledge you acquire more actionable.

As important as it is to learn continuously, it is equally crucial to maintain a balanced approach. Overindulgence in learning can lead to burnout and disengagement. Pace yourself and strive for a balanced life where learning complements rather than overwhelms your existing responsibilities. Prioritise quality learning experiences over quantity, focusing on those that truly enrich your life and resonate with your values.

For those who may feel intimidated by the prospect of lifelong learning, consider starting small. Integrate small, manageable learning into your day-to-day life. This could be as simple as listening to podcasts, enrolling in a short workshop or dedicating fifteen minutes a day to reading. As you develop a rhythm and discover what forms of learning you enjoy, you can gradually expand your efforts. Remember that each step counts, and progress is made in iterations rather than leaps.

The Power of Becoming

Embracing continuous learning also means welcoming the notion of failure as a necessary part of the process. In our immediate gratification culture, we may feel pressured to perform perfectly or succeed swiftly. However, meaningful growth often emerges from the lessons learned through setbacks. Develop a mind-set that sees challenges as valuable feedback, whether in the form of mistakes in a project, a failed attempt at a new skill, or criticism of your work. By reframing failure as an opportunity for reflection and learning, you cultivate resilience that will serve you in various aspects of life.

Setting educational goals can be a powerful motivator on your lifelong learning journey. Consider what you want to achieve in the short and long term. Do you wish to change careers, obtain a new certification or develop a personal project? Clearly defined goals provide direction and a sense of purpose. Break these goals down into smaller, actionable steps to make them more attainable.

Celebrate your achievements along the way to reinforce your commitment to learning; this will keep you motivated and help you appreciate the progress you make.

As you embark on this journey of continuous learning, do not forget to find joy in the process. Entrepreneurship, creativity and genuine transformation stem from a place of enthusiasm and passion. Allow your interests to guide your learning; passions will ignite curiosity, making the process feel less like a chore and more like an adventure.

As you explore various learning avenues, stay attuned to the potential of interdisciplinary connections. Knowledge from seemingly unrelated fields can often provide fresh insights and innovative solutions. Consider how principles from psychology might deepen your understanding of leadership or how art can inspire creativity in your professional endeavours. By crossing traditional boundaries of learning, you expand your capacity to innovate and adapt, enhancing your sense of self-efficacy.

Finally, engaging with a community of fellow learners can profoundly enhance your lifelong learning journey. Whether through book clubs, study groups or online forums, sharing ideas and insights with others can rekindle your enthusiasm for learning. Engaging discussions often spark new avenues of exploration and deepen your understanding of complex subjects. The encouragement, accountability and inspiration that come from a supportive learning community can make all the difference in maintaining your momentum.

Embracing continuous learning is akin to embracing a lifelong journey of becoming. In redefining your relationship with education and knowledge, you create a resilient foundation for yourself. Recognising that learning is not solely about accumulation but a dynamic, evolving process expands your understanding of who you are and who you can become. As you cultivate curiosity, nurture your passions and engage with others along the way, you lay the groundwork not just for achieving personal and professional goals, but for crafting a life rich with purpose, meaning and ongoing transformation.

In the end, the power of continuous learning serves as both a catalyst and companion on your unique journey of becoming. Each lesson learned becomes a stepping stone on the path to the best version of yourself. As you take the next step, whether that is picking up a new book, signing up for a course or connecting with someone new, remember that the journey of becoming is a lifelong process.

Embrace it with open arms, knowing that each new insight and every moment of learning brings you closer to the best self you aspire to be. Celebrate the progress made, remain open to opportunities for growth and carry the torch of curiosity and learning throughout your life's journey.

Celebrating Your Journey

The concept of celebration is often overlooked in the pursuit of growth, yet it plays a crucial role in sustaining motivation and fostering a sense of fulfilment. Each step we take on our journey of becoming carries significance, no matter how small it may seem. When we learn to acknowledge and celebrate these small wins, we cultivate an environment where our transformation can thrive.

As we traverse our personal growth paths, it is vital to take time to appreciate the milestones, those moments of progress that indicate we are moving forward. Celebrating small wins is not merely about pausing to revel in our achievements; it is about recognising the effort, dedication and resilience that each victory represents. These moments act as reminders that we are indeed transforming and evolving, emboldening us to forge ahead with renewed vigour.

The initial step in celebrating our journey is developing self-awareness. Reflecting upon our paths allows us to recognise our growth. Most often, we are so focused on the final destination that we forget to acknowledge the steps we have taken to get there. This leads to a skewed perception of progress, in which we only feel satisfaction when we hit significant milestones. However, the real magic lies in the smaller achievements that accumulate over time, building momentum that fuels our journey.

Consider maintaining a success journal or a gratitude list where you document every accomplishment, regardless of size. This practice not only helps you track your progress; it also reinforces a positive mind-set and sparks appreciation for the work you put in daily. When each entry in your journal reflects not just achievements but also realisations, lessons learned and moments of courage, it becomes a powerful testament to your journey.

Integrating gratitude into our everyday lives is another fundamental aspect of celebrating our journey. Gratitude transforms our perspective and sharpens our focus on the positive aspects of our experiences, highlighting all that we have learned and achieved. When we deliberately express gratitude for the small wins, we bolster our emotional well-being and create a cycle of positivity that can propel us forward.

Practising gratitude can be as simple as taking a moment each day to reflect on what went well. This ritual can shift our attention from the burdens of challenges to the blessings within our journey. Expressing gratitude helps us develop a sense of contentment and joy in our evolution, understanding that we are not merely chasing goals but experiencing life. Try setting aside a few minutes each evening to jot down three things you are grateful for. Over time, this simple exercise can deepen your appreciation for growth and remind you that every step counts.

Celebration does not have to be extravagant; it can be as simple as sharing your achievements with a friend, treating yourself to a favourite snack or taking a moment to bask in the pride of your effort. The act of celebrating reinforces the notion that every part of your journey is worthwhile. It builds a positive association with your growth, shaping a mind-set that embraces challenges rather than fearing them.

Moreover, acknowledging small wins cultivates resilience. The journey to becoming our best selves is rarely linear. There will be plateaus and setbacks, moments when progress feels stagnant or elusive. Celebrating small victories during these times becomes even more crucial, acting as a buoy that keeps us afloat when the waters become choppy. It reminds us that even during challenging periods, we have made strides. Each small win, even the effort to keep moving forward amid adversity, deserves recognition.

Building a culture of celebration can also spread to the people around us. Sharing our victories with others builds community and fosters connections. When we celebrate our achievements, we inspire those in our lives to acknowledge their journeys as well. This communal aspect can create a ripple effect, inspiring others to recognise their own progress and encouraging each other to keep moving forward.

Consider organising gatherings where you and your friends or co-workers share achievements from the past month, no matter how big or small. These celebrations can strengthen bonds and create an uplifting atmosphere where everyone feels motivated to embrace their journeys. This practice encourages open dialogue about growth, allowing individuals to express both struggles and triumphs, fostering mutual support and accountability.

Additionally, finding creative ways to celebrate can renew our enthusiasm and zest for the journey. Whether it is hosting a themed party for personal milestones, enjoying a special outing, or simply taking time to engage in a favourite hobby, creativity can foster joyful moments that punctuate our progress. Celebrating in novel ways stimulates excitement about the journey and reinforces our commitment to personal evolution.

As we recognise and appreciate our small wins, we must also cultivate a mind-set that fosters reflection. Reflection is not just about looking back but about understanding how we have grown from our experiences. It presents us with the opportunity to analyse what worked, what did not and what adjustments we can make going forward. Regularly reviewing our progress can deepen our understanding of ourselves and strengthen our connection to our journey.

One powerful reflection practice is conducting a monthly review. Set aside time at the end of each month to evaluate your accomplishments, progress, detours and insights gained. This habit allows you to chart your evolution over time, encouraging a broad view of your growth journey. It can also prepare you to set intentional goals for the next month, establishing the groundwork for future wins.

Furthermore, it is essential to be mindful of comparison during our journeys. In a digitally driven world, it is easy to fall into the trap of measuring progress against others. However, celebrating your journey means focusing on your unique path. Comparisons can cloud our judgement regarding our achievements, hindering our ability to recognise the significance of our small victories.

Instead, aim to view your journey through your own lens. Celebrate the uniqueness of your experiences, acknowledging that they contribute to your individuality. Personal growth is not a race; it is a lifelong commitment to flourish as our authentic selves. When we honour our stories and remain focused on our inspiration, we cultivate an unwavering sense of determination that enriches our transformation journey.

In the mosaic of our life journeys, each piece, each small win, plays a vital role in creating an expansive and beautiful picture. Embracing this theme not only helps us understand our growth but also encourages us to maintain the motivation to strive for our best selves. Remember, the journey of becoming is an adventure meant to be relished, filled with learning, exploration and precious moments of self-discovery.

As you continue on your path of becoming, I encourage you to carve out time to celebrate. Celebrate the effort, celebrate the challenges overcome, the lessons learned and the small yet mighty steps forward. Create rituals that resonate with you, recognising that every small victory is a foundation for the grander achievements to come. In and of itself, your journey is a testament to your strength, resilience and commitment to living your best life.

Ultimately, celebrating your journey is an act of love, a love for yourself and your growth. It acknowledges that becoming is not solely about what you achieve but also about who you become along the way. Embrace the journey, honour each step and remember that every win, no matter how small, brings you closer to your true self.Inviting Others to Grow with You

As we journey through life, we often discover that growth is not merely a solitary endeavour. While our paths may be deeply personal, the importance of community and connection cannot be overstated. In the context of "becoming," inviting others to grow with you enriches not only your own experiences but also nurtures the growth of those around you. It creates a tapestry woven from diverse strands of aspirations, vulnerabilities and strengths, ultimately leading to a more profound understanding of ourselves and our collective potential.

To foster a community of growth, we first need to embrace the idea that each individual carries their own potential. This belief enables us to see the light in others and reinforces a culture of encouragement. When we genuinely invite others to join us on our journeys of self-improvement, we not only offer our support but also create an environment where they feel valued and empowered to pursue their own dreams. By recognising the unique contributions each person brings, we begin to create a rich ecosystem that thrives on mutual growth.

One practical way to invite others to grow with us is through sharing our journeys transparently. This vulnerability cultivates trust, which is fundamental in establishing supportive relationships. When we freely share our struggles and triumphs, we help others see that they are not alone in their challenges. It is essential to create spaces where everyone feels safe to express their feelings, whether it is joy, frustration or fear. This openness encourages dialogue, allowing others to feel comfortable sharing their experiences and aspirations.

In any community, there will naturally be varying levels of confidence and progress. To facilitate growth among your peers, it is essential to actively listen and show compassion. Listening not only validates the experiences of others but also opens the door to understanding their viewpoints and needs. By practising empathetic listening, we can help others articulate their thoughts and feelings more clearly, guiding them through their own discoveries. This involves holding space for them, asking insightful questions and fostering a spirit of exploration.

Another technique for inviting others to grow with you is to set collective intentions. By having group discussions that delve into personal and shared goals, community members can align their aspirations with one another. When individuals articulate their core values and dreams, it becomes easier to identify common threads that bind the group together. Whether it is through workshops, brainstorming sessions or casual gatherings, fostering an environment where collective intentions are set empowers members to feel connected to one another's journeys.

In practice, setting collective intentions can manifest in numerous ways, such as book clubs that explore personal development literature, study groups focusing on specific skills or community projects that align with shared passions. Such initiatives reinforce the belief that growth is a collaborative effort. Members can come together to celebrate not only individual milestones but also group achievements, thus nurturing the idea that every step forward is a triumph for all.

Celebration plays a pivotal role in sustaining motivation and commitment within the group. It is vital to recognise and celebrate even the smallest victories within your community. By doing so, we create an atmosphere where progress feels tangible and worth acknowledging. Throwing small gatherings or creating a "brag board" where members can share their achievements can reinforce the idea that every contribution matters. This fosters a culture of positivity that encourages others to pursue their own paths with renewed enthusiasm.

Furthermore, mentoring relationships are a powerful method of inviting others to grow alongside us. Engaging in informal mentorship, where experienced individuals guide those who may be newer or less confident in their journeys, can have profound effects on both parties. The mentor gains insights from the mentee's fresh perspective, while the mentee benefits from the wisdom and guidance of someone who has navigated similar challenges. Establishing these relationships can create a robust support network, amplifying the growth experience for everyone involved.

To effectively mentor others, it is essential to cultivate patience and understanding. Not everyone will grow at the same pace, and that is OK. Recognise that each individual has different experiences, learning styles and emotional responses. Providing encouragement rather than imposing expectations allows for a more organic and supportive growth process. By remaining approachable and open-minded, we can inspire others to chart their paths while feeling confident in their uniqueness.

In any community focused on growth, challenges will inevitably arise. Conflicts, misunderstandings and setbacks may occur, frequently testing the bonds of connection and support. It is during these times that a growth-centric community must exhibit resilience. Take the opportunity to address issues openly, emphasising clear communication and seeking solutions together. Encouraging members to voice their concerns and work through conflicts collaboratively strengthens the foundation of the community.

The Power of Becoming

To promote conflict resolution, establish ground rules for discussions that prioritise respect and understanding. Encourage a solutions-oriented approach, where members are invited to participate in brainstorming sessions aimed at resolving conflicts. This not only helps the individuals involved but also allows the community to learn and grow together, reinforcing the collective commitment to supporting one another.

Reinforcing accountability is another essential aspect of fostering a growth-oriented community. While it is crucial to uplift each other, it is equally important to hold one another responsible for progress. Setting measurable goals and regularly checking in on each other fosters a sense of accountability and shared commitment. This can be done through peer accountability groups where members share their objectives, discuss challenges and celebrate progress together.

To facilitate this process further, implementing a structured goal-setting framework can be beneficial. For instance, using the SMART criteria (Specific, Measurable, Achievable, Relevant, Time-bound) can guide individuals in defining their personal goals while ensuring that they remain accountable to the community. Periodic check-ins, whether weekly or monthly, allow members to reflect on their progress and regroup to adjust their strategies if needed.

Additionally, expanding our definition of success within the community fosters growth when we celebrate varied achievements. Success is not a one-size-fits-all concept. By recognising diverse forms of progress, whether mastering a new skill, overcoming a fear or simply showing up each day, community members are encouraged to honour their journeys. This validation fosters motivation and boosts confidence, allowing everyone to appreciate their efforts as they cultivate a more robust sense of self.

Moreover, bringing in guest speakers or facilitators to lead workshops can provide fresh insights and perspectives that spark growth within the community. Experts who specialise in areas of interest, whether mindfulness, leadership or creativity, can share their knowledge and inspire group members to expand their horizons. These external inputs can stimulate conversations and motivate individuals to step outside their comfort zones, broadening their understanding of themselves and the world.

Creating a culture of sharing resources is an additional way to invite growth. Encourage community members to share books, articles, podcasts or online courses that resonate with their journeys. By cultivating an atmosphere where resources are freely exchanged, members can embark on new learning experiences and expand their perspectives, discovering valuable insights that contribute to their personal development.

As we extend invitations for others to grow with us, it is important to remember the significance of gratitude. Expressing appreciation for the contributions of others strengthens community bonds and fosters an environment where individuals feel valued. Regularly sharing words of encouragement, writing thank-you notes or acknowledging others' efforts in group settings can reinforce connections and motivate members to continue supporting one another on their respective journeys.

Gratitude should not be merely a reactive outcome but should be integrated into the community culture. Consider implementing gratitude practices, such as sharing three things you are grateful for

The Power of Becoming

at the beginning of a gathering or creating a gratitude wall where members can post notes appreciating one another. By embedding gratitude into the fabric of the community, individuals are empowered to recognise and celebrate the positive impact they have on each other's lives.

Finally, extending the invitation to grow with others allows us to create a legacy of transformation that resonates beyond our immediate community. As individuals embark on their growth journeys and share their insights with others, they inspire a ripple effect that reaches far and wide. Encouraging personal development in others can lead to widespread change, fostering a culture of support, resilience and growth that transcends generations.

To truly embody the spirit of inviting others to grow with us, we must continually remind ourselves that each person we touch has the potential to inspire someone else. When we focus on empowering others, we foster a collective momentum that enriches everyone's journey, culminating in a powerful network of like-minded individuals committed to personal and community growth.

In conclusion, inviting others to grow with us is a fundamental aspect of "becoming" that requires intention, empathy and commitment. By cultivating a supportive community that values openness, accountability and gratitude, we nurture an environment where everyone feels inspired to embark on their growth journeys. As individuals continue to evolve and thrive together, we lay the groundwork for a more connected and empowered world, enriching both our lives and those of countless others.

Embrace the call to invite others, knowing that we are all interconnected in this magnificent journey of becoming. Together, we can illuminate the path forward, celebrating growth in all its diverse forms and transforming not only ourselves but the world around us, one act of invitation at a time.